PRISM OF LOVE

Daniel J. O'Leary

Prism of Love

GOD'S COLOURS IN EVERYDAY LIFE

the columba press

First published in 2003 by
the columba press
55A Spruce Avenue, Stillorgan Industrial Park,
Blackrock, Co Dublin

Cover by Gerry Symes and Bill Bolger
Origination by The Columba Press
Printed in Ireland by ColourBooks Ltd, Dublin
Repinted 2009

ISBN 1 85607 404 8

Acknowledgements

To the people of Ripon, North Yorkshire, for welcoming me into their city and into their lives in the first year of this third millennium. May all the citizens, and especially the children, of this proud and ancient 'Cathedral City to the Yorkshire Dales' be forever blessed.

To all the readers of my previous book, *Travelling Light*. So many have written to me and encouraged me to keep grappling with the mystery. They have invited me to their homes, their communities and their countries.

To Linda Marsh for dreaming up the title of this book and, together with Margaret Siberry, for providing constant inspiration and guidance throughout the two years it took to complete. To David McAndrew who proof-read the text and offered excellent advice. To my friend Fr Jim and the parishioners of St Wilfrid's for their affirmation and trust.

To Steve, Jean, Diane (am) and Diane (pm) of Acrill Newspapers, Yorkshire (incl. *The Ripon Gazette*), for commissioning most of these reflections. These friends were all a joy to work with and they have enriched my life.

Finally, *Prism of Love* has come to birth because of the waves of compassion and wisdom that are beginning to flow, ever more powerfully, across the brave souls of those who, no matter what the cost, or what the state of our institutions, desire to live the free and abundant life promised to them by the Son of Man, the Human One.

Contents

Your one shining moment
Do you ever revisit it?

Into every life, the wise ones say, comes one shining moment. It is a moment of glory. The curtains part, the vision is granted, and something is changed forever. That single experience, in one way or another, stays with us always and colours the whole of our lives. It is the timeless time when the veil is drawn from the mystery of our existence, when our essence is disclosed to us, when we discover – even if only fleetingly – who we really are. It is a highly personal 'moment of truth'.

Your one bright and shining moment may have to do with naming what, or who, you really love; with revealing to you the job or the relationship that is slowly destroying you; with becoming aware that all your decisions and reactions spring from a deeply hidden anxiety, anger or fear; that you need no longer be afraid because you are loved unconditionally by a God who delights in you; that, without a doubt, the universe and life itself are safe places for yourself, your children and all you love; that everything that has ever happened to you was not random happen-chance but part of a carefully crafted love story; that God comes to you usually disguised as your life, in all its bits and pieces; that apart from one or two cherished beliefs, nothing matters very much; that it is in our weakness and sinfulness that we are strongest of all; that we are indestructible and untouchable as long as we remain close to God.

In his short life with us, there were many shafts of brightness, we can be sure, of immense significance for Jesus. In the dark light of his desert temptations there was a lot of shining. In his encounters with the women in his life, there was much disclosure. We remember, for instance, his insights about the eternal meaning in the sacrificial moment of the widow's penny, his peerless communion in the transparent moment of exchange with the woman at the well, his human self-revelation in the intimate moments with Mary and Martha. He spoke of the threshold-instant when the casements of all our hearts would fly open for us to behold the traffic of angels between heaven and earth. And he certainly had an amazingly close encounter with a light from another place on the mountain of his transfiguration.

The human life of Jesus in time and space was one of the brightest shining moments in the history of creation. In the fullness and totality of his very own humanity lies the secret passage to the heart of God. And, therefore, likewise with us. It is during our most desperate, ecstatic, despairing, joyful, routine, hopeless times that those luminous moments of clarity surround us with stunning transparency. We are held in a threshold between two phases of our lives – not to do with the chronological time of years and decades but with the *kairos*-time of falling into mystery, of falling in love with God. These moments heal and transcend the damaging religious education of our childhood days and liberate us into the belief that we are all gods-in-the-making, that even from our murkiest and most sinful encounters with evil, God can bring light.

R. S. Thomas, one of our finest poets, died a few years ago. He wrote about life's moments. He was drawn to the story that Jesus told about the person who glimpsed a piece of the mystery – and who then went on to buy the field with the treasure in it (Mt 13:44). In *The Bright Field* he moulds and shapes into 14 lines, so much scriptural imagery, so much of our traditional Catholic theology of childhood and of the mystics' spirituality of creation. And he does this in a way that echoes all over our hearts, bringing memories of moments whose light will never go out:

I have seen the sun break through
to illuminate a small field
for a while, and gone my way
and forgotten it. But that was the pearl
of great price, the one field that had
the treasure in it. I realise now
that I must give all that I have
to possess it. Life is not hurrying
on to a receding future, nor hankering after
an imagined past. It is the turning
aside like Moses to the miracle
of the lit bush, to a brightness
that seemed as transitory as your youth
once, but is the eternity that awaits you.

Faces of your soul
How many of them do you know?

Do you ever surprise yourself at what you notice going on inside you? Think of times during the past few weeks when you seemed to be a different person from your usual, familiar self. Do you remember times of sudden outrage, of deep loss, of intense delight, of hatred, of jealousy, of fear? Reflect for a moment on the strength of those moods and emotions, those highs and lows, those secret desires, fantasies and restlessness? Sometimes it seems as though there are different people living inside us.

One night a few weeks ago, for instance, I had the face of a potential killer as, in panic and fear, I chased an intruder around the presbytery. I scared both myself and the thief at the ferocity of my rage and the obscenity of my language. Soon afterwards, under a mild enough threat, I wore the face of a coward. Within days, a surge of grace had my eyes shining with hope and vision. Later again, rocked by temptation, my face was bereft of strength.

We are taken aback, even shocked, by the various characters that emerge and take their turn on the stage of each of our days. Sometimes it is the saint who comes to the fore, or the sinner, the hero or heroine, the wild man or wild woman, the hunter or huntress, the harlot, the seducer, the conscientious mother or father, the good Catholic. I have listened to parents who were amazed at the rage they felt towards their children, their spouses, even wishing them dead and then feeling guilty for ages afterwards. Holy people have talked to me about the temptations that filled their nights, the blasphemies that filled their days.

Yet all those forceful feelings are part of us. We dare not deny their existence and their influence over us. If we suppress and try to bury them, they will eventually destroy us. They are all faces of who we are. They are the community of our heart. We are called to accept them and to hold them. We bring them all – the weeds and the wheat, in the imagery of Jesus – before ourselves and before God in meditation, and before our special friends in honest intimacy. To pretend that we are all light, living

perfectly in the state of perpetual grace, is to live a lie that dam-
ages our soul. The greater the gift, the greater the shadow.
Enlightenment happens, not in the light, but when the darkness
prevails.

Those moments when we think and act and feel emotions
that are unfamiliar, out of character, alien to our normal, pat-
terned way of life – such moments carry huge secrets to facilitate
our breakthrough into the real self, into how we save our souls.
In fact these are the times when we learn most about what is
going on within us. The danger is, as Rainer Maria Rilke said,
that when our devils are driven out, our angels leave as well.
They are the supreme moments of true awareness, ready to dis-
close their treasures of wisdom to open hearts.

We are rarely told about how much Jesus learned from his
shadow side – from the outrage, the anger, the temptations, the
doubts that plagued his life. In the dark light of his desert temptations we see one of his many faces. In his encounters with the
women in his life, we see many more. To Mary and Martha he
revealed the face of his need for human intimacy. On his day of
anger in the temple, he showed the world his face of outrage.
The transfiguration provided him and us with the terrible beauty
of his hidden divinity. His face of despair stares at us from the
Cross.

But whatever face he showed, it was the face of God. So too
with us. Because Jesus lived through all the experiences of humanity, wearing all the faces possible for a human being to
wear, they are all, if we but believe it, redemptive for our souls.
We take our masks, our scars, our shadow to heaven with us.
Only there, they will be shining. In the meantime, here in this
world, the challenge to us is, not to do battle with our many
faces, but to be aware of them. In God's economy, they too have
a place in the grand scheme of things.

For Christ plays in ten thousand places,
lovely in limbs, and lovely in eyes not his
to the Father, through the features
of men's faces. (G. M. Hopkins)

Everything Belongs
The same good energy runs through all life

I was walking by the obelisk in the Market Square on my way to
Boots for another supply of St John's Wort. My mood wasn't
great. The sudden floods had thwarted me all morning in my
efforts to visit some parishioners. It was now bucketing it down.
I had a small hole in my shoe. And I had forgotten my cap. Like
a child I was whining, 'Why are you picking on me, O nasty
God?'

That was the moment I saw it – a tiny, fragile snow-drop
peeping out at the base of the giant, eternal obelisk. It was like a
gift from heaven. It went straight to my soul. 'Take heart, Daniel,'
it seemed to say, 'have you not noticed that Spring is on the
way?'

That was the turning-point. The snow-drop had put the
Spring in my step. My mood changed. Soon I began to notice all
kinds of little miracles happening around me. The following day
I was driving north to comfort a bereaved family. Even while
slushy snow was still lingering in high headlands, I could not
miss the first delicate sheen of green wheat and barley across the
brown, newly-furrowed fields. And again my heart lifted.

What is occurring to me now is how much a part of nature
we all are. Spring happens in our bodies as well as in our fields.
As the days get longer, our spirits get lighter. When the country-
side around us renews itself these weeks, so too our hearts are
empowered. It is the same energy that runs through everything.

Dylan Thomas refers to the intimate interplay of relationship
between the universe, our own hearts and God.
The force that through the green fuse drives the flower
Drives my green age ...
The force that drives the water through the rocks
Drives my red blood.

I began to understand how everything is related to everything else. Everything is connected. Everything belongs in the
bigger picture. Tread on a daisy and trouble a star! The heartbeat
of every living thing beats in our hearts too. And they all beat in
the heart of God. Or, put more accurately, we could say, 'If we

listen with our whole spirit, we can hear the heart-beat of God in everything that lives – and that includes the music from a rock.' This is a marvellous mystery and we humans are in the middle of it.

When the sun rises over our city and its surrounding fields, our spirits become glad as well. We look at the sea from the lighthouse and something deep lights up within us. We walk on the moors and the dales and our souls come alive. And, in the evening, and we sit near the fire with a glass of wine, we are filled with those special memories that bring smiles and tears.

And even while the cold rain slices against our windows, already, in a warmer place, a little swallow is getting ready for her long flight to our shores.

Pausing for breath
We have a choice about our moods and feelings

It is three-thirty pm. I'm at the check-out in Safeways. I'm irritable and feeling sorry for myself. Its been a difficult day, so far. All morning, everyone seems to be having a go at me. My feet are cold. Its snowing outside. Now its getting too hot inside. And the man ahead of me in the queue is paying for his half-pound of sausages by some complicated method that requires him to sign three documents. I'm inwardly fuming; I have so much to do before evening, yet I'm trying to force a brittle smile at one or two of our parishioners. Little do they know about the awful things going on in my mind!

So, before I scream, fall over, have a heart-attack or hit someone, what do I do? I still have just enough room in my head, and energy in my heart, to stop the rot and to change the direction of my thoughts and feelings. I then do a few very simple things. In the first place I stand up straight and take a few deep breaths. Ah! that's better. Already my shoulders are beginning to drop and my body relaxes a little. What a relief! I had become all tense and stiff. Every joint was locked rigidly. So I rocked a bit on my feet. Ever so slightly; ever so gently.

Then I began to think differently about what was going on inside me. Why was I making myself so unhappy? Why was I blaming everyone today – God for the snow, Safeways for the heat, the poor man in front of me for holding me up? 'This is crazy,' I said to myself. 'All this negative thinking is only damaging my own peace of mind. If I don't stop this now I'll make myself even more unhappy and I'll be impossible to live with when I get home.'

So I began to think about all the good things in my life. My cold, for instance, is getting better. I'm beginning to forget about my recent break-in. I got a compliment yesterday, last week the doctor gave me a clean bill of health, my friends care about me, I'm getting used to my new glasses, my car does not need a new radiator after all. Then I remembered how I used to love the snow as a boy in Ireland, how I loved the warmth of our small grocery shop on a cold day, how this delay at the check-out is giving me the chance to pause for a moment and say a prayer of thanks to God that I'm alive and able to walk around the Market Place this Thursday afternoon, enjoying all the bargains and banter of this marvellous city.

What is happening to me is a growing awareness of the choices I have about how I live and feel each day. I imagine a line running across my mind, separating my thoughts. Below the line are the murky waters of complaining, fretting and anxiety. Above the line is where the positive and hopeful energies are waiting to be tapped into.

It is at this point that I have a choice. I can remain a victim of my own negativity and descend into the self-perpetuating distress of the touchy ego. Or I can reach out of that swampy place and find that firm and life-giving ground of positive thinking and letting go. This is now a daily habit that brings me untold relief. It is like escaping from a suffocating and moody cellar into God's fresh air.

So, God is good. Enjoy today. You have a choice about how you spend it. It is up to you.

Everything is holy
God is always already there

It is Thursday morning at nine o'clock. I'm walking along Church Lane. The place is thronged with people and cars in front of the three adjacent nursery/primary schools. Some mothers look grim; others so happy. Some of the children are ecstatic; others pouting and resisting. I sense the range of struggling emotions going on inside them – the hopes, disappointments, delight and fear.

Later on I'm walking through the Thursday Market stalls, tables and displays in the town quare. All of life is there, too. The farmers are fearful, the locals are conversing, the sellers are expectant. Locally made artefacts and home-made organic produce offer a wholesome and homely atmosphere to savour. It is good to be here; to feel I belong in this urban, classless crowd that is moving around this homely place.

On my way home I pass the City Centre Surgery. Worried parents are hurrying in with their pale children; others are emerging with relief on their faces – the news of the x-ray or biopsy must have been good; and there are some with a terrible fear in their eyes. In some way I felt a part of them all; I found it easy to share their anxiety and relief.

Further down the road I had to visit the Police Station to make a delayed statement about the burglary at the presbytery. While I was waiting there, near the desk, I heard some of the comments of those visitors who were caught for speeding, for drink-driving offences, for assault or theft – many of their livelihoods now in shreds.

Late that night I sat down, exhausted. At 64 I get tired so quickly now. I asked myself a question: 'As a Christian priest, what have I to say to all those people I saw around the city today? I had the privilege of glimpsing something of the mystery of their human hearts – the highs and lows, the light and darkness. What, if anything, do I have to offer?'

Only this. 'Your lives are already full of God. You do not need to go anywhere else to find God. God is at your fingertips when you feed and dress your children, wipe their bottoms, and

stroke them to sleep. God is in your feet when you drag yourself
to another day of boring work, or rush to a friend's party. God is
in your mouth when you try to say a consoling word of encouragement. When your heart beats faster in hope or desperation, it
is God's heart beating within you. When you break down and
weep, it is God who is weeping inside you. Whether you know it
not, God is always already there.'

How do I know this? I know it because that is what Jesus
came to reveal to us. Nothing more; nothing less. We are always
loved extravagantly by a Mother-God. God cannot remember
our sins or forget our beauty. We are utterly divine and we do
not know it; we are full of God's loveliness and we don't believe
it; we can heal each other as Jesus did, but nobody told us.

And even if we were told such astonishing stories, such
amazing good news, we would scarcely believe it. Because we
are so unfamiliar with unconditional love in our own lives, we
cannot accept that it can ever happen to us. We have a strange
resistance to this chance of intimacy with God. This, then, is why
we need to go to church on Sunday; why we celebrate the eucharist each week and say our prayers – so that we will never
forget, that what I have just told you, is true.

In praise of praise
When I affirm you, I, too, grow

I don't like the fog. It shuts out the light. Last week we had an old-fashioned pea-souper around our town when you could hardly see your hand. I got lost driving home from my brother's parish in Manchester. I hate getting lost and I'm always doing it. 'But how,' you might ask, 'could anyone get lost on that straight-forward journey? There's a huge sign for the M1 North off the M62. You'd have to be a special kind of idiot to miss that!' Yet I did. God help me, I did. I drove up to the presbytery feeling really sorry for myself. Still fearful since my recent break-in, as I turned the key in the door I thought, 'What a glorious night for burglars.' I switched on the news. The foot and mouth disease was still spreading. New rumours of war. These were my dark thoughts as I got ready for bed.

The phone rang. An old friend. 'How are you, Daniel?' 'Never better,' I lied. But soon I told her the truth about feeling down and miserable. My friend then gently reminded me of some good things that I had recently done, some positive comments she had heard about me, and that she believed in me and valued our friendship. On hearing such affirmation and encouragement I immediately perked up. The fog seemed to lift, at least from my heart. I thought about the power of genuine praise. It can heal our souls and renew our self-esteem. It can bring us hope. It can enable us to believe in the dawn even while it is still dark; to trust the light even in the dark fog. The words of a song, given to me by my mother many decades ago, came back to my mind.

> *If with pleasure you are viewing*
> *Any work that I am doing,*
> *If you like me or you love me tell me now.*
> *Don't withold your affirmation*
> *Till the priest makes his oration*
> *And I lie with snowy lilies o'er my brow.*
> *If I earn your praise, bestow it; if you dig me let me know it,*
> *Let the words of true encouragement be said.*
> *Do not wait till life is over and I'm underneath the clover,*
> *For I cannot read my tombstone when I'm dead.*

We often need reminding about the Celtic belief that everything we send out comes back three-fold. When we think or talk in a mean way, our souls shrivel. When we curse someone, the curse returns to damage ourselves. And when we praise, our own hearts swell with a healthy self-esteem. There is no thought, word or act of generosity that does not, sooner or later, enrich the giver. It is well-kept secret.

Could we, I wonder, have a 'Praise Somebody Today' week here in the parish? This would be a week free from grumbling, grousing and complaining. Maybe the week after Easter Sunday. We would tell people what we enjoy about them. Or how well they do something. I don't mean empty or false flattery. I mean real, wholesome affirmation and true praise. I think it would make a big difference. Even stressed-out people would be walking around our streets with huge smiles on their faces. The energy of the city would change. It would be like the first Easter all over again.

Losing the rag
Your anger has long roots in the past

Road-rage! Not me. I don't do road-rage. Or so I thought. Until one day I'm driving down from the presbytery on to Main Street. It is a very narrow road. To be on the safe side, I drive (illegally) with my two left-side wheels on the pavement. A car passes and there's a small crack as it clips my wing-mirror. That does it. I snap. I shout some very nasty words. And now I'm in a bad mood.

When the rage passes I do some serious thinking about my sudden emotions. During the next few days I try to notice my reactions to the daily happenings in my life. It amazes me how often I get uptight and irritated. I'm drumming the table with impatience just because someone is slow in coming to the phone. I'm ready to explode just because on the one day I decide not to take my anorak, it rains!

And, as I continue to keep an eye on my feelings and moods, the list of times when I tend to 'fly off the handle' continues to grow. Maybe not in any violent sense but, nevertheless, I have to admit to some kind of waiting-in-the queue rage, trolley-in-the-ankle-rage, getting-the-ansafone-again rage, dogs-not-on-a-lease rage. I am truly surprised at this because, in general, I would have called myself a fairly even-tempered fellow. I never fail to be surprised at how little I really know about myself. It is only lately, as I'm given the disturbing grace of penetrating my practised disguises, that I'm beginning to squirm at the extent to which others can see, even more clearly, through my cracked masks.

But why am I like this? Am I the only one with an inner fuse waiting to be lit? Or are we all going around with a hidden anger in us? And how do these over-the-top reactions affect the people we are with? What does it do to our blood-pressure? Apart from plain selfishness and the stress of each day, there is another special reason for our bizarre behaviour.

Most of our extreme emotional reactions are connected with events from our past, especially our childhood. I fly into a fury at some slight provocation because of the number of times I've had to repress my anger a long time ago. My anger, for instance, at the clip on my car-mirror may have triggered off the suppressed anger at the bishop who clipped my wings when I was a young curate, or the teacher who clipped my ear when I was a boy. Or parents may shout at their children because, when small, they themselves were forced to keep silent when their own parents were shouting at them.

I began to realise more and more that there is a strong connection between my extreme behaviour now, and what happened to me when I was small. Again, for instance, when I burst into tears for no apparent reason, maybe at a funeral or at someone else's sad story, it may well be directly connected to all the un-mourned moments in my past decades – the funerals I was never taken to as a child, the tears I was never allowed to shed, the grief I was supposed to suppress. And being a boy, it was seen as weak to cry.

As I continue to think about these things, my life becomes more and more interesting. The next time someone clips your wing-mirror or, as happens every day, someone 'rubs you up the wrong way', try to reflect a little on your reaction. Maybe such an unlikely moment offers you a way of understanding the mystery of yourself a little more.

The impossible dream
The importance of believing in yourself

I'm well past mid-life now. I'm also getting flash-backs from my earlier decades. Sometimes its like looking at a video of my life – the happy times, the painful times, the empty times. What I notice a lot is the fact that I've almost always followed my dream. I'm pleased about that. Wherever there was a choice, I have always 'gone for it'.

One part of me – the voice of my parents, teachers, priests – would advise me to 'play it safe', to 'kick for touch', to be careful and cautious. But the stronger voice would encourage me to take the risk, to listen to my heart, to trust in my angels, to feel the fear and do it anyway!

What I found really interesting was this: every time I pursued my dream, every time I gave my best energy and talents to achieving something good and beautiful, there were always lots of people trying to stop me. Someone always wanted to pull me down, to dash my ideals. They still do.

I wonder about this. What makes people be like that? Why do they want to destroy what is beautiful? And it does not happen to me only. It is probably your story too. Maybe it is the story of everybody who tries to be different, to add a little colour to life, to break the deadly monotony and boredom of each day's living.

So why do we wish bad things on those who try to do good things? Is it envy? Is it jealousy? Is there something deep and unhappy within us that wants darkness rather than light, lies rather than truth, ugliness rather than beauty, conflict rather than peace?

Last week we gathered in the Market Place to remember what happened to Jesus. His dream was crucified too. Because he was a good and beautiful man, he was stalked, hunted down and finally destroyed. There seems to be no exception. The best of our stories, dramas, films and music are created from the lives of those men and women who have watched the crucifixion of their own lovely dreams. Most of our tears begin to flow, it is said, when we see the difference between the dreams we once had for our lives, and the way we have since turned out to be.

And so I ask myself, 'Is that the end, then? If so many people are stuck in the mud, fearful of change, full of hate towards those who follow the dreams of their heart – is it not better, then, to forget those dreams, to settle for less, to compromise like everyone else?'

Please believe me, the answer is No. Continue to trust your heart, to follow your dearest hopes. No matter what your age, all you ever wished for is still possible. There is no impossible dream. Your heart can only tell the truth. In the long run, it will not deceive you. You were created for goodness, for truth and for beauty. With God's power in you, everything is possible.

'I can do all things in him who makes me strong.' Only fear stayed nailed to the Cross. Once he had come away from it, Jesus greeted Mary and the disciples with the life-giving words 'Fear not.'

Every morning we need to whisper this message to our anxious hearts: Do not be afraid for I have redeemed you. I have called you by your name. You are mine. When you take on the swirling rapids, as I hope you will; you will not drown. When you walk through the leaping flames, as one day you must, you will not be harmed. You are the apple of my eye. You are so very precious in my sight. I have carved your name in the palms of my hand. Your name is 'My Delight', 'My Beloved', 'My Betrothed'. (Isaiah)

A God who never gives up on us
Something good in the worst of us and ...

He was a young man. He was crouched over the wet mud in the dug-up Market Place. Very intently, he was scraping away the dirt from every deeply-embedded stone. In his hand was something that looked like a small spoon. Most of the stuff he would throw away, but every now and then he paid special attention to some tiny fragment, placing it carefully to one side. 'Excuse me, what are you doing?' I ventured to ask him. Graciously he explained. 'I'm an archaeologist from Durham University,' he said, 'and I'm trying to find something of value here; something worth keeping.'

As I crossed the road to Woolworth's for a passport photograph, I was smiling to myself. I was remembering the words – 'something of value; something worth keeping.' In my mind's eye I saw myself, after I had died, thrown out of heaven by St Peter, as a piece of worthless scrap, unfit to live with the saints. Then I saw God running out through the pearly gates, bending down over me, with a small spoon, like the university student in the Market Place.

So there was God, carefully sifting and scraping through my life, throwing away the dirt and the mistakes and the sins. I could hear God whispering, 'There must be something of value here; something worth keeping. Even if it kills me (again!), I'll find the golden part of Daniel, the shiny bit that is made in my own image. Even Daniel cannot destroy that!'

I was smiling because this image of God was not the one I was brought up with. As a child I was told about a hard God, who searched for my bad bits, not my good bits; a God of fear rather than of joy. I was smiling because I do not believe any more in a God who punishes – only in a God who loves and laughs and weeps. These days I only believe in a God who never, ever gives up on me.

And I also believe that there is nothing without its own strange beauty. Because existence means life, and life means God, then it must follow that there is something divine even in the least attractive of things. For some strange reason I find these words of Ralph Emerson both amusing and reassuring:

Let me go where'er I will, I hear a sky-born music still;
it sounds from all things old;
it sounds from all things young ,
from all that's fair, from all that's foul,
peals out a cheerful song.

It is not only in the rose, it is not only in the bird,
not only where the rainbow glows,
nor in the song of woman heard;
but in the darkest, meanest things
there alway, alway, something sings.

'Tis not in highest stars alone, nor in the cups of budding flowers,
nor in the red-breast's mellow tone,
nor in the bow that smiles in showers.
But in the mud and scum of things,
there alway, alway, something sings.

God's ways are not ours
You can transform your self-pity

Golf at 11.00am That was the main item in my diary for Bank Holiday Monday. I was really looking forward to it, after a busy few weeks. No appointments, no meetings, no long services. The day dawned bright and warm. But I woke up to a dreadful flu. (Men don't have mere colds; it is always a heavy flu!) Here I was, definitely deserving a hard-earned day-off and, at the last moment, it was snatched from me.

Inwardly I fussed and fumed, blamed God, blamed everyone and everything. To comfort myself I went down to Harry Bell's for a fish-and-chips. The queue there was too long. More curses. As I stormed my way to Safeways for a sandwich, I noticed that people in their shorts and T-shirts were looking at me in a funny kind of way. Then I realised that, because I felt so cold, I had put on my winter jacket and a corduroy cap! 'Oh! what a crappy Bank Holiday!' was all I could think of.

Back at the presbytery I took myself in hand. I poured out a glass of wine and spoke to myself in this way: 'Daniel, stop acting the martyr. You're being a right pain. You're acting like a spoiled child, making yourself out to be an innocent victim. For God's sake, let go of the self-pity and try to enjoy what's left of the day.'

So I sat back, put my feet up, took a few deep breaths, let my tense shoulders drop, and, for the first time that day, began to feel a little more human and civilised. As I began to reflect on my Oscar-winning performance up to that point of the day, three things came into my mind.

The first was about how lucky I was to have my health, to be able to hold down a job, and to have the friends who were worrying about me, even at that very time. With a shock I recognised those priceless gifts that I am always, and so insensitively, taking for granted. I made a quiet decision to try to be more grateful for the hidden blessings that fill my life.

The second thought I had was about my expectations for the Bank Holiday. I began to realise that it was my unfulfilled plans that brought me so much grief and disappointment. The

Buddhists and the Hindus believe that all suffering comes from our expectations and over-attachments to people, projects or things. Being so human and so needy, I suppose we cannot help building up our hopes. When they are dashed, we are so let down. I began to realise how much of my life was based on such expectations and often-unrealistic hopes.

My third reflection was about the fact that there may be a special reason for today's disappointment, a greater design at work in my life than my own limited efforts. Maybe something more advantageous than my own golf plans would happen to me today. My Mom, observing my way of living my life, would sometimes suddenly ask me, 'How do you make God laugh?' Each time I would silently shake my head. 'Tell him your plans for yourself!' she would whisper.

It is never too late
To make the dream that you are come true

Visiting retirement and nursing homes in and around the parish is part of the pastoral ministry of a priest. Sometimes I find it difficult. It brings back memories of my own mother who died at 97 two years ago. Occasionally, too, I get a telling-off from those who disagree with something I have written in a newspaper, or in the parish newsletter. Only last week I was taken to task for not wearing my Roman collar!

But overall, it is a most enriching experience. What I like most of all is listening to the stories of those elderly people about the important moments of their lives. Suddenly, during a fairly routine conversation with someone who may seem to be nodding off, a gem of memory will emerge like a pearl from an oyster. 'Oh yes, didn't you know? I was a famous ballet-dancer. I travelled the world. My toes are all twisted now from it but, in my day, I was the best.'

Or, as on another day, an eighty-year-old man shyly uncovered a collection of his rally-driving trophies. 'We were competitive, but we were friends. It was the hardest life. There was less glamour about racing cars in those days. But winning was wonderful.' There are many more accounts of magic moments and magic lives, dreams that came true and dreams that were denied. Only last week I buried a man who rode many winners in famous races. He winked as he said, 'I was very popular with the clergy'. Next week's funeral here in the parish is for a former Tiller Girl. I was there when she was dying and wondered if her dancing days were soon to start again. Some stories are true; some are fantasies. (In a sense, does it really matter?)

The mystics say that God dreams a dream in all of us when we're born. God hopes that one day our lives will fulfil that dream. Most of us lose the dream as we get older, or someone steals it from us. That is why we cry – when we see the distance between the dream we were born with and what we have turned out to be.

'Life breaks everybody,' wrote Ernest Hemingway, 'and some people grow at the broken places.' But not all do. It is so sad to see the bitterness, the fretfulness and the emptiness of so many elderly people. The hurts of life, the wounds of failure, the pain of rejection, the bad memories of our past lives – all of these can destroy the soul.

The followers of Jesus say that even though, for whatever reason, God's dream may seem to have died within us, it is never completely lost. It can always be regained. New life can be breathed into it. At any age, the recovery of the dream is possible. At any age our inner divinity can shine through.

Is there a secret dream in your heart today – a dream you have kept hidden even from yourself? Is there any *real* reason for not taking the risk to pursue that dream? The alternative is to do nothing, and so to miss something beautiful happening in your life.

We find it so hard to believe that with God's power everything is possible. Some people dare to believe it and their lives are changed forever. And your age has nothing to do with it. Your holy and beautiful heart is always young. It will not mislead you. Listen to it.

Taking time out
Can you find the still point in your crowded day?

I was watching Ireland fighting for her life in a recent rugby encounter with 'the ould enemy'! I was as limp as an empty glove
when the game was over. Ireland won. But why was I so intense,
so competitive, so desperately involved? At one stage in the game,
I actually added my 175 kilos to the scrum in an effort to heave
the ball across the line! Luckily I was on my own! That was the
moment when I came to my senses. I asked myself a few basic
questions.

Since there was nothing in it personally for me, why was I so
anxious about the outcome of the game? Where does this overwhelming desire to win come from? Am I this way about everything? When does the drive to win stop? When will I accept the
way things are, without always trying to control the outcome? Is
it a man's thing to always want to be on the winning side? Are
women less compelled to beat someone down?

I think of the competitive way I drive my car. For instance,
depending on my mood, if somebody tries to overtake me, I
sometimes find myself increasing my speed to avoid being
passed. Not very clever. Or somebody tells a story or a joke. I try
to tell a better one. This one-up-manship is all rather futile and
can ruin a conversation between friends. The more I become
aware of the way I think and talk, the more surprised I am at the
vanity and envy I find in my life.

It is during the quiet time I spend each morning that I realise
much about myself. Before the city gets moving I meditate a little on what is going on in my life and in the lives of those around
me. These days I'm trying to accept who I am without always
striving to be different; to go with the flow of my life without
forcing its speed to increase; to stop trying to control people and
outcomes and to trust more in the presence of God; to believe
that it is enough to be fully present to those around me, to do my
work as well as I can, and to notice the colours of the flowers and
of the city.

Without this quiet time each morning I would make more
mistakes each day. It is the special time when I come face to face

with my emotional drives and compulsions, with my bad habits and repeated mistakes, with my ability for missing some of the important and precious moments that happen around me. Many mornings I wake up and forget to greet the sun, to thank God for another day in which to meet my friends, to enjoy the taste of porridge and the sound of children, to see the joys and pain of the next 24 hours as pure gift.

Interestingly, men and women who have no time for religion or formal prayer believe passionately in the importance of setting aside 15 or 20 minutes each day to review their lives, their inner composure, their attitudes to their colleagues, their prejudices and fears, their greed and carelessness, and their gifts too. Without developing a deep and gentle awareness of ourselves and our emotional reactions, we may miss the abundant, joy-filled life of which, with God's help, we are all capable.

Morning affirmation
Or how to face another day

There are mornings when I leap out of bed, full of energy, eager to get to grips with whatever the day will offer. There are other mornings when I don't want to get up. Everything seems too much. I panic at the thought of the work to get through, the difficult people to cope with, the expectations to meet.

These expectations can become a real block – the expectations of others who want me to be the kind of pastor, or friend, or colleague they want; my own expectations as I push myself, and others, too hard. Some mornings, all of this can become quite unbearable. I allow myself to become a victim of these controlling thoughts and influences. It makes me feel tired of trying to please, of proving that I'm good enough. I want to turn over and refuse to get up. Stop the world, I want to get off!

Then I think of other people with far more demands and pressures than I have. Parents of young children, for instance, with the whole world of work that happens every morning – the feeding, the peace-making, the ferrying to school, the early shopping – all before getting to work themselves. Parents may be suffering from a cold, a depression, bad news or real anxiety – but they must keep going; they cannot ring up sick or go back to bed. There are many others for whom each day is a challenge to their physical and mental stamina.

This is the moment when I call on the power of God to restore peace to my soul, new energy to my body, joy to my heart. I surrender to a higher power. I hand over control of my day to the Mystery of Life. I try to trust more. To do this I need my daily 15 minutes of silent time. It helps to quieten my mind and my racing thoughts; to face my worries and fears, and then calmly to let go of them.

When I was small, in our Catholic school near Killarney, I was told that each one of us had our own guardian angel, a special friend of God whose job it was to look after me in particular. I was also told that the ancient Celts would draw an imaginary ring of protective light around them before the day began, to shield and guard them from the dangerous and hurtful forces that lay ahead.

Each morning I think of these things. A lovely prayer called *The Breastplate of St Patrick* begins with the words 'I will arise today with the mighty strength of the Creator of Creation.' When I pray like this I find a great peace and freedom flooding my soul. I feel God's power inside me. My fears don't seem so strong and crippling anymore. 'In the middle of my winter I find an invincible summer.'

I stop being a victim. I stop giving permission to people and circumstances to control my life and to decide my moods. This is when I allow my shoulders to relax, when I breathe more easily and deeply, when a new courage lifts my head and runs through my body.

Whatever you can do, or dream you can, begin it.

Boldness has genius, power and magic in it. (Goethe)

The flow of life
Everything does not depend on you!

To London by train or to London by road? That was my dilemma last weekend. Pressed for time, behind with work, dead-lines looming, conflicting priorities – so I decided to drive. By burning it up on the M1, late on Sunday evening, I would gain a little time after Mass to prepare for my Monday morning conference at Mill Hill. 'Yes,' I said to myself, 'I can control my panic in this way.'

As I was making these frenzied decisions I received a phone-call. Another friend of mine was in the ICU of Leeds Infirmary. A minor heart-attack. (Is there such a thing as a minor heart-attack?) He had joined the growing list of my colleagues who, because of burn-out, slight strokes, depression and various forms of intensive stress, have had to take time out to recuperate (if they're lucky!).

Every now and then, even in our busiest times, a moment of insight can come. On that day last week I had one such moment of clarity – when the scales fell from my eyes, the veils parted, and I saw a little into the reality of things. I suddenly began to realise what an utter idiot I was. Risking life and limb, my own and others, by pushing a clapped-out old banger at 80mph in a very tired and distracted state of mind – and all for what? – to fulfil a commitment I could easily have refused in the first place.

What is ironic is this. I talk and write a lot about pacing yourself, about going with the flow, about taking your heavy foot off the pedal of life, about cooling the pace so as to stop and smell the flowers. And yet I nearly lost the plot myself. Because you cannot go with the flow in the fast lane – the fast lane is a driven place. You cannot let go in a motorway macho-race – you are gripping the wheel too tightly. You cannot let yourself be carried when you're 'in the driver's seat'. You cannot reflect on the state of your soul when you're screaming at the slow-coach road-hog in front of you, and the mad driver behind you is riding on your rear bumper.

So I went by train. I booked a seat with a table (£1 extra). That is where I'm sitting now, as I write these words that you are so

gracious to read. With a can of Guinness in one hand and my
pen in the other, I'm almost at peace with myself and the world.
Through the window, the flying fields are green, the day is so
warm, and the seat across from me is vacant, thank God. So I've
said a few prayers, I feel ready for tomorrow's challenge, I'm
breathing easily and relaxing my shoulders for the first time
today.

And then I hear them whispering in heaven: 'I think the stub-
born old fool has finally got it.'

Soul-space
A few guidelines for happiness

I have just made my bi-annual 'retreat'; that is, I spent a few days completely on my own, re-charging my spiritual batteries. If I do not examine my own life, and my own shadow-stuff, how can I be of any use to you, our readers, or to those who listen to me each week?

There is a story about the European bounty-hunter in Africa who was trying to get his loot and booty across the country to the coast before the rains came. One morning, his native Kenyan helpers refused to pick up his boxes, bags and trunks of gold and elephant tusks. He bullied, threatened and bribed them. They still refused. He finally got the message. 'They were waiting,' they said, 'for their souls to catch up.'

I often feel like this. It is easy to lose one's soul. Like St Paul, having preached to others, I myself may well become a castaway. Without the benefit of a wife and family to keep me grounded, rounded and centred, I need to do what many of you would probably love to do – find a quiet place to pray. At such times I reflect on guidelines for happiness and 'things to try':

- Decide to be happy. Learn to find pleasure in little things;
- Life is always a mixed bag – like Basset's Allsorts or Cadbury's Roses. Each day brings a mixture of emotions. Life is like that. Nobody promised us a rose garden;
- You cannot please everyone. Don't cling to your failures. Learn to keep letting go of all anxiety:
- Learn to laugh at yourself. You are not the centre of the universe. Don't take yourself too seriously. Look at the bigger picture. Trust in God and in your friends;
- Be your own person. Do not let yourself be anyone else's victim. It is not possible to live up to the expectations of other people. You only have to account to yourself and God;
- You carry God's dream for your happiness within you. It is a dream about your freedom from fear. If you really want to, you can make that dream come true;
- Do not be controlled by the negative voices of your parents, your teachers and the religious leaders of your childhood. They are tapes from the past, they keep playing in our heads;

- Trust in God's extravagant love for you. Fill your mind with lovely thoughts – compassionate and generous. You may feel the fear – but do it anyway! You are well protected at all times, whether you know it or not, by the angels of God;
- Think of others. Jesus, and all our greatest women and men reminded us of this saving grace. Because our hearts are made to grow by forgetting themselves, we become happier the more we take care of others;
- Live for today; there is only the present moment. Life is short enough. Enjoy every second of your one, wild and precious life. And may God love and bless you always.

Living life to the full
Do you ever feel another kind of hunger?

I watch a lot of sport on TV. Recently I watched some of the Wimbledon tennis. Those men and women were so fit, fast and focused. I marvelled at their quickness of hand and eye, their grace and speed and power. To reach this level of performance, to achieve this mastery of their art, they had to dedicate their whole lives.

Having switched off the TV, I ask myself a question: 'To what achievement or pursuit am I as committed as they are? To win what goal do I have such a passion? Into what work do I pour my best efforts and energy?' Many answers run through my head. I try hard to be a good pastor to my people, to raise money for our future building needs, to keep my friendships in good repair, to keep abreast of all that is evolving in my chosen profession. Probably much the same is true for you – your devotion to your partner, to your children, to your health, your home, your work and promotion, your social life and hobbies.

'But isn't there more?' I ask myself. 'Is that all there is?' What I'm getting at is this. We all have an amazing capacity within us for joy and delight; a potential for happiness and freedom; a gift for healing and liberating ourselves and others from depression, anxiety and fear. We have a hunger for a deeper, richer way of living that includes, but is greater than all the work, duties and responsibilities that fill our days and nights. We carry dreams within us from childhood; we have a soul that will live on for ever; we are each an image of God's beauty. So what are we doing about these powerful promptings of our spirit?

The Wimbledon athletes touch the limits of their potential as tennis-players. They develop those talents and gifts to the highest degree possible, even though the applause and sense of triumph does not last long. At great personal cost they discipline and hone their bodies and skills to near-perfection. And the very few lucky ones will cherish their fleeting hour of glory.

I firmly believe, dear reader, that at much less cost, a deep peace is available to all of us. We are created to enjoy such happiness. It does not mean that our lives will be without suffering.

But it does mean that we can always break through our darkness. The glory of God, the Christian believes, is each one of us fully alive (not half-alive). Jesus came that we might live the abundant life (not just merely exist).

All we have to do to enjoy this delightful way of living is to ask God for it earnestly (maybe during your 15 minutes quiet time each morning or evening). And remember that God is called our 'Tremendous Lover' whose constant delight is to fill us with love, excitement and peace.

Heroes of the heart
For many champions, the applause comes later

I love athletics. I even have many trophies from a past millennium. (To the click of my Mom's rosary beads, as she prayed by the finishing tape, I helped Gneeveguilla Athletic Club to a hard-fought victory in the All-Ireland 50+ veteran 100 metres Relay in Cork in 1993!) Another World Athletics Championships is due to begin soon. Grace and power will be the order of the day. Records will be broken and new champions will be crowned. The sporting world will hold its breath.

Yet I sometimes wonder about it all. Are we rewarding and adoring the most deserving people? What about the unsung heroes and heroines whose hidden service of our local community is so vital? Are we applauding only the physically spectacular, ignoring those unknown and devoted 'stars' who nourish the differently-abled among us?

What I mean is this. In the sports pages over the next few weeks, we will read about the fastest, but not about the most patient; about the highest, but not about the most humble; about the strongest, but not about the most vulnerable; about the fittest, but not about the wisest; about the most competitive, but not about the most compassionate; about the glory, but not about the cross.

During the last Olympic Games, Fr Colm Kilcoyne writes, a nurse was speaking about the excitement of the competition. She painted pictures of the triumph of the winners as they stood on the podium, wearing their medals, the roar of the crowd in their ears. Then she shifted the scene to the children's hospital where she worked.

She talked about the sick child she cared for. He had serious bone trouble in his legs, and could not walk. For months this nurse had worked patiently with him, trying to get the power back into the frail little legs. She was also whispering courage into his anxious heart.

One day she had him balanced, yet again, on his familiar support-frame. Maybe this would be the moment she dreamed of – the moment he would move on his own. She had prayed with him, she loved him, she now willed him into taking a step. And suddenly, he did – he took *one step*. Just then, distracted by the noise on the TV, the nurse looked up from his flushed, excited little face to see an Olympic champion on the victory stage, pumping the air in triumph as he stood on the victory stand – before a full stadium and a watching world.

However, there was nobody around to witness the boy's victory, except his nurse. Yet his one small step had been as great as the giant stride of the record-breaking athlete. But no cameras, no medals. Just a small boy who had taken one faltering step, and then fallen into the arms of his nurse – a nurse who would not trade that moment for all the gold in all the Olympic medals ever minted.

In the stillness is the dancing
Only in silence does love emerge

A busy young mother came to see me last week. We were talking about the importance of some quiet moments each day. She told me that she had experienced a moment of intense wonder while breast-feeding her baby on a cliff near the sea, during one of our recent warm afternoons. A most profound understanding about her life had come to her in that moment of silence. Lovers know all about this, as do the contemplative religious orders.

Many people long for a moment of silence each day. So do I. Without it, I'm like a car without a steering wheel. I'm capable of causing immense damage because I'm not balanced in my heart. I hurt people because I'm not still and quiet enough to hear them properly, to grasp the deeper meaning of what they're saying.

It is at times of fear that I need the space and silence to cope with the pressing panic. This is the time for gathering my angels around me, for trying to get things into perspective, for letting my shoulders drop and taking a few slow, measured breaths. It is the time when I stop running away from the fear in my life, when I stand to encounter it face to face, because, so often it turns out that my fear is all a figment of my own imagination, with no reality behind it.

At the root of my fear and of my need for silence is the reassurance that I am truly loved. There is a story that I play over in my mind every so often, to convince me of how precious I am to God and to others. It is a picture of a mother waiting at her window for her children to be dropped off by the school bus and come rushing up the driveway.

She reaches for a chair to lean on while she watches them, dishevelled and untidy, socks around their ankles, ties and ribbons askew, buttons undone, faces smudged from the fall-out of the day's adventures. Excited and laughing they run to the front door. The mother leans forward on the chair-back to track them to the very end. She also leans on the chair because her heart is so aching with intense love that her knees are going weak.

That is one of the images that never fails to restore my courage at a weak moment. That is how God sees and loves me –

and you. So many of us were never told about that beautiful God when we were small – only about a vengeful God who made a hell and who punishes people. It is a terrible sin to teach and preach like that – and many still do.

Love drives away fear. When we know we are loved, we walk tall and can face the darkness with a new heart. And only in silence does the true meaning of love emerge.

To be nobody else
On being able to say 'It is all right to be me'

It was a warm day in San Francisco. The workshop was intensive. Our group was exploring the source of the inner pressures of our lives. For some it was anger, for some more it was anxiety, for others it was painful memories, or revenge, or envy, or a variety of negative attitudes and emotions.

The greatest number of people, however, (and the majority of them were women) said that their greatest suffering came from trying to satisfy the expectations of others. Feeling 'not good enough' was the heartfelt cry of this group. They felt used, exploited and victimised by those they worked for, or lived with.

They deeply resented being trapped into other people's agendas, having to prove themselves worthy – and always being judged as not coming up to scratch. The inevitable result of all of this was a loss of self-respect and self-esteem. They longed to be accepted for what they actually were. This group inwardly rebelled against being measured up against others, being compared (unfavourably) with their colleagues, expected to be 'perfect' rather than truly themselves.

I'm sure there are many of you 'out there' who feel like this. I do. Whether it comes from our bosses, our partners, our colleagues, our neighbours or our wider families, few of us escape the unwelcome scrutiny. Even in an age of gender-awareness, women's liberation and increased all-round equality, there are subtle pressures on most of us to conform, to perform, to compete and to prove.

Maybe some of this is good. Maybe at times we need to be challenged, to be pushed, to be critiqued. But there is a deeply destructive danger to our souls when we feel we 'must get it right' all the time, when we always feel judged, compared and disapproved of.

This is how we lose our inner spirit, how our soul is betrayed, how our joy in life is destroyed. For many in that special USA, West Coast group, once they realised what was going on in their lives, a breakthrough happened. After some delicate sharing, most of them began to set themselves free of all those ever-present expectations.

They began to realise that it was more important to be honest rather than to be always trying too hard, to be at ease with themselves rather than to be straining to impress, to be self-accepting rather than always competing, to be authentic rather than to be perfect.

Our life's quest is not to be perfect but to be aware of, and to accept our imperfection. God says to us 'Come as you are. Because I made you, you are beautiful. Let no one steal that vision from you.'

Are you in your element?
Because when you are, you are aflame with God

Benedict was a hopeless student. I know, because I taught him. He failed all his exams; he drank too much; he was a lazy waster; he just did not fit into university life. But on the rugby pitch he was pure magic. Like quick-silver he shimmied and dummied, dropped a shoulder, changed direction and was over for a try. Or, again, delicately poised, he would turn on a sixpence, and with exquisite balance, release an impossible drop-kick. On the field, Ben was in his element.

My brother Joseph was a Down's Syndrome person. Joseph moved to a different drummer – sometimes out of step, sometimes awkward. But once the music began to play, Joseph was transformed. Oblivious of all else except his body's unique intimacy with the rhythm, he moved with stunning grace and beauty. When dancing, our Joseph was in his element.

Rainer Maria Rilke is a lovely poet. He wrote about the ungainly way that a swan walks and waddles to the river. It is not a pretty sight. But once in the water, something beautiful happens. Everything is changed. In calm elegance the lumbering swan is poetry in motion, now carried by the water. She is in her element.

Have you ever seen the often-shown classic Yorkshire film *Kes*? It is about a Barnsley boy, always in trouble and an inveterate sloucher, totally out of kilter in the school scene, whose passion and soul stirred for a bird – the kestrel he tamed and in which he found a meaning for his life. With his beloved Kes, he was in his element.

One more example. By accident, an eagle's egg, fallen from its high nest, was hatched by a family of prairie chickens. It grew up within this environment, hopping and scratching, limited and stuck. One morning a majestic eagle soared over the scorched desert of this earth-bound family. The adopted chicken felt an aching intimacy with this mighty and powerful heroine of the skies. 'Stop it,' the prairie hens shrieked, 'don't even think about it, you fool. You're not an eagle; you're a prairie chicken. Just you hop, scratch and stay stuck, like us, for the rest of your life.'

Now that I'm older, I can identify those shared moments when I'm not stuck, when I know that I'm at my best, at my most authentic – those moments for which I believe I was created, the sacred times when I'm in my element. Can you, dear reader, at whatever age you may be, identify those experiences in your ever-changing life, when you know that this is what you really are destined for, when you are at one with the flow of life inside you, when you feel truly free?

I only write about these things because I believe there is something wonderfully healing and life-giving about being able to name and claim those special and holy parts of our daily lives when we shine like the sun, when we are truly in our element. Maybe this is what St Paul meant when he wrote about bringing our 'hidden self' out into the open so that it may transform our own life, the life of our friends and enemies, the life of our country and planet.

All human life is there
There are many levels in our complex lives

Last week I cut up the *The Independent* into book-sized pages. For a euro or two I had bought the equivalent of a fairly robust novel. Within its pages, and written large, were all the plots and stories of the human heart. There were accounts of the high aspirations and low intrigues of our citizens, their hopes and fears, their successes and failures, their crimes and their compassion. I sat down for a few minutes' reflection and thought: this is like the diary of my own life; in these pages is my story too; it is not about 'them out there' and 'me in here' – there is a part of me in every item of news in this paper.

Later, as I watched *News at Ten*, I wondered how we ever manage to cope with the fascinating, and sometimes horrifying, range of human achievements and destruction that are graphically thrust into our living-rooms and into our fragile minds and vulnerable hearts each evening. How do we contain and grapple with these emotional and evocative images and stories about the powers we possess to damage each other so much, or to set each other free in a new way?

There is a part of us that is drawn towards the darkness. But there is always a part of us that is thirsting for what is truly beautiful; a part of us that will be nourished only by the most uplifting and liberating challenges.

As we read and watch the events of the world within the intimacy of our homes each day, I believe that we are touched at very deep levels of our soul. Because we are all human beings, with amazing powers for good and evil, many of us are quite affected by the media, whether we are reading the sensational hype of the tabloids, or watching the bland fare of so much television.

In the same way, as we move around our towns, looking for a parking space, rushing to get some shopping done, trying not to bump into anybody bigger than ourselves, we are all, I believe, travelling another and deeper journey at the same time. There is a searching going on within us for a more enduring kind of joy. Beyond the routine of so much of our lives there is a beauty and mystery that is waiting to be discovered.

To keep us aware of that inner seeking is why I write these Reflections – to try to touch that often-neglected, under-nourished and quite divine part of us; that part of us that carries our finest aspirations and without which we will surely die. We forever need to be reminded that we come from God (or whatever name we give to the mystery of our existence) and that back to God we will one day go.

I write, in the first place, to convince myself. But it is wonderful, too, to be acknowledged and affirmed. I want to thank all those of you who have confirmed me in my convictions and efforts so far. You have been marvellous in your generosity. Your remarks have given me a new heart and a new hope.

The mystery of the moment
Do you notice the miracles all around you?

In front of me heaves the Atlantic. The huge waves break at my feet. I'm sitting, dreaming, in my favourite spot along the south-west coast of Ireland. Next parish is in Newfoundland! I'm relaxed and reflecting – my first real break since arriving in my new parish one year ago.

One of my favourite themes for these Reflections is that of the hidden richness of our lives. Nothing is really dull, ordinary or uninteresting. Everything is a source of wonder and beauty, if we could but slow down enough to appreciate what surrounds us.

Just a moment ago I was having a snack. A very dishevelled and unkempt old man placed a dirty black box by my side and asked me to keep an eye on it while he went to the toilet. My judging mind went into overdrive. Was he dangerous? Was this a bomb? What was he up to? He returned, thanked me gently, removed an instrument from the box, sat down at the front-door and played some soul-stirring tunes on his button-accordion. A crowd gathered quietly around him.

It is all too easy to be blinded by fear and suspicion. Too often we are not present to the richness, graces and blessings of our days and nights. Because of the stresses and strains of our work and families, we are seldom aware of what is going on, seldom inside ourselves enough to savour the flavour of the everyday routines. I believe that many of our readers are trying to live their lives at this deeper level.

Our search for fulfilment, or for love, or for meaning, or for God usually takes us towards something or someone outside ourselves, beyond our present experiences. What we find it difficult to believe is that we can easily find within us what we seek so desperately somewhere else.

The trick is how to live in the present, how to be aware of what is just below the surface of our lives, how to come home to ourselves. God and joy do not have to be searched out and found. They are already here. But we need to be in the here and now too.

Sometimes we have to be shocked into this realisation, this new way of being and seeing. Very often it is only when our health, wealth or family is suddenly threatened that the penny drops, that we realise all the beauty and wonder we take for granted.

Victor Frankl, a famous philosopher and writer, was declared clinically dead for a short while. When his life was restored to him he wrote: 'Suddenly everything gets precious, gets piercingly important. You get stabbed by things – by flowers and babies and by beautiful things; just the very act of living, of walking and breathing, of eating, having friends and chatting. Suddenly there are miracles everywhere.'

My brother's keeper
Do you ever feel guilty?

'Sorry, I've no change!' That's what I said to the young man selling *The Big Issue* outside Woolworth's. I then went into W. H. Smith's to buy a thrashy novel. I felt guilty afterwards. Every Saturday a few itinerants come to my door. Whenever I fob them off with money rather than a little time to chat over a cup of tea, I feel guilty too.

Scarcely a week passes without a number of 'begging letters' arriving on my desk. They are all for good causes – OXFAM, CAFOD, SHELTER, MIND, LIFE, etc. Sometimes I reach for my personal cheque-book; mostly I don't; but always – that guilty feeling.

From my comfortable chair in front of the TV I look at the atrocious ways that people are treating each other. So much greed and hatred. It happens at home and abroad. It happens in politics, in religion and in our own neighbourhood. I always feel that I'm not doing my bit to alleviate at least some of this unnecessary misery. Yet I continue with my cosy life, hoping that a few prayers, a few quid and a few cast-offs will ease my conscience. I wonder what other people feel?

I want these Reflections to be upbeat and positive, but also realistic and searching. There is no way we can avoid being affected and disturbed by the relentlessly shocking daily News, followed by those adverts pleading for our help. How do we decide what to do? Do we give a lot to some, or a little to all, or nothing to anybody? And whose fault is it anyway that so much neediness exists?

Could good management and careful government, we ask, have avoided so much starvation, exploitation and mass-murder? Why should we, who have worked hard for our personal comforts, have to worry about those addicts who, through their own fault, sleep rough on our streets? Just because we happen to live in the West, why should we have to bail others out, to pick up the tab for careless husbandry, offer asylum to all and sundry?

I wish I knew! There are many good answers to such questions.

Most religions and denominations, for instance, are quite clear about our duty to our neighbour. And most decent folk help others out at times. But, in general, so much within us wants to follow a different and tighter path – a self-protective one. When it comes to our time and our money, charity certainly begins at home – and usually stays there!

Strangely enough, of one thing I am sure. The more I give away, even reluctantly, the more enriched my heart becomes. The more freely I give, the luckier I get! An ancient Celtic piece of wisdom reminds us that every precious thing we let go of is returned to us threefold.

Instincts of the heart
We have a homing device for heaven in our soul

Autumn is a powerful season. I think we all die a little during its strange evenings. Something goes out of us. Maybe that is why it is such a poignant moment when the swallows fly away. A few weeks ago, by the Lakes of Killarney, I watched them gathering, just before the warm evenings began to grow cold. In breath-taking unison they swooped and swerved, drawn and driven by their own inner radar. Perched on roof-tops and telephone wires, they would pause for a timeless moment of perfect silence, and then, as one, they would rise into the skies and begin their journey for southern shores.

Children seem to understand something of 'the swallow's intuition'. In my sister's school the pupils reflected on how the birds knew when to go, how to find their way to North Africa, and, next year, when to return to the very same tree in the playground of the school. Many loving messages were written to the swallows: 'Goodbye, we will miss you', 'Travel safely to your sunny destination', 'Please come back when the summer's in the meadows'.

We have, in Ireland, a story about a special child. 'Little Owen of the Swallows' was dying. No one knew why. One autumn day he told his mother that he would be leaving home forever with his winged friends. The local people sensed some strange bond between the boy and the birds. It was evening when Owen was sitting on some rocks, as the October winds were coming in from the sea. As the cloud of swallows set off for brighter places, one of them swung around, and back and down, and brushed, with its wing, the big tears from the small pale face of the dying boy. His bewildered mother, watching through the window, was weeping too.

As I reflected on the homing instincts of the swallows, on how unerringly and naturally coded they are to find their place in the sun, to reach their final and true destination, it was but a small step for me to shift my heart and mind from the flight of the swallows to our own journey through the countries and seasons of our lives. I believe that our human hearts, too, carry an inner kind of wiring. They are coded for Love, and programmed for God.

In spite of the distractions and temptations of a very materialistic and greedy world, in spite of our personal sins and betrayals, in spite of our disappointment and disillusion with our secular and religious leaders, there is still a homing device within us that remembers the source of our life and our love, that recognises that eternal place of our origin and destiny, and that guides us, like the swallows, safely home.

Saying yes to life

Do you always choose 'life to the full' over mere existence?

Last Saturday evening I watched the Parkinson programme. The Readings at the Vigil Mass were a bit depressing and the rumours of war were spreading. I needed a break so I switched on to old Parky. His guests were Elton John, George Best and the Beckhams.

They all spoke of their weird and wonderful lives, of their failures, their addictions, and the hate-mail and death-threats they had received. Their brilliant careers had lots of bleak spaces. Their amazing gifts carried equally striking shadows. They had all reached their breaking-points and, more than once, had considered the awful and ultimate escape of self-destruction. They were familiar with tragedy; they were acquainted with grief.

As their stories were told and the labyrinths of their lives were revealed, I was filled with admiration. Yes, I know that they all have their critics and begrudgers. Don't we all. Yes, they have too much money, they brought their own disasters on themselves, only their own fecklessness to blame. But they are all survivors. They refused to give up. They chose life. Their light was stronger than their darkness. They were beaten to the ground but they came back to stand tall once again.

They have reached heights and depths that most will never know anything about. Millions have enjoyed them, loved them, envied them, hated them. They have shone like shooting stars; they have plummeted like falling stars. They have known both intense glory and humiliating defeat. But, like beacons of hope, enriched by their suffering, refined by the extremes of their excesses and vulnerability, they were honestly and openly chatting away there with Parky.

I know we have guaranteed role-models that we turn to when the chips are down. We have St Wilfrid and Mother Teresa and St Cuthbert. But they often seem to be too remote from the stresses and strains, the terrorism and temptations of this third millennium. You may well have little time for the people I write about. But I did feel better after the programme. I felt a surge of grace. If they can do it, so can I. If they can face their demons and transform them into gifts, then so can I. If they can live to tell the tale, if they can grow through their personal sins, failures, tragedies, then so can I.

God works in mysterious ways. Everyone and everything can be a source of divine blessing, a window of wonder on a God of Surprises. There is an inner power, a Higher Self at work in all of us – healing, loving, reassuring, comforting, encouraging, empowering. There is no pit out of which we cannot climb; no rut that cannot be re-routed.

With God at its centre, the human spirit is indomitable. It thrives in adversity. 'In the middle of my winter,' wrote the poet, 'I discovered an invincible summer.'

The tears of things
There are intimations of mortality all around us

What a welcome surprise – a brief Indian Summer of sorts in mid-October. Just when we thought the warm days had gone with the swallows. How our hearts and bodies rejoiced in the sun! Nevertheless, Autumn is now here and it, too, is welcome. It has an important part to play in the turning of the seasons. While Spring touches our bodies with its new life, Autumn, I think, touches our hearts. This 'fall' of the year seems to cast a haunting spell over our lives. These days, at the feel of the mist on our cheek as we leave for work, or at the drop of a leaf as we walk home, Autumn works a strange magic in the depths of our soul.

Around Yorkshire's famous Fountains Abbey, for instance, where I now live, the numinous quality of the fog and the winds, the smells and colours of woods and fields, the texture of the morning and evening skies, all carry some inexpressible intimations of another home, another barely-glimpsed country. What is so heart-wrenching is our half-remembered sense of intimacy with a long-forgotten place inside us. It is as though a part of us was once familiar with another world, and now, something about autumn stillness whispers life into those timeless, slumbering memories.

Small wonder that the oldest and greatest cultures and religions of the world celebrate the realities of life and death, of gods and goddesses, of mystery and paradox, during the dim days of Autumn. It is the time that we visit our cemeteries and pray for the dead. As the November Christian feasts of All Saints and All Souls perennially remind us, we are drawn into mystery when we celebrate the journey of souls from this world to the next. The Celtic rituals of *Samhain* (next week) contained the most amazing ceremonies and traditions to help people cope with the mysterious traffic between the world and the underworld, between gods and humans, darkness and light.

On a still Autumn evening, when the light has a quality you never noticed before, echoes of eternity steal into your soul, bringing disturbing longings for what we cannot describe. It is also a melancholy moment, with tinges of loss and of 'the tears of things'. I sometimes think that of all the Autumns in our lives, there is one that is extra-special – the most poignant of all. It can happen to us at any age – as an open-hearted child, as a broken-hearted teenager, at the crises of mid-life, or in our last, precious decades.

I'm writing about that one Autumn in our lives when the veil parts and we see, for one shining moment, into the beauty of God. This is a moment of disclosure – an aching, memory-laden moment. It is a time to take off your shoes. You are touching another world. You hold your breath. When this happens to you, you know, beyond all doubt, that death is not the end; that you are saved forever.

Fear of the dark
There is really nothing to fear; fear, in fact, is a gift

'I'm afraid of the dark!' What a confession for a fully-grown man to make! I believe in ghosts, too. I live in a strange old house full of spooky noises at night. A few weeks ago I was watching a fairly ordinary video. I had to switch it off and headed swiftly for the bed. Like when I was a child, I felt safer with the blankets over my head.

Sensitive to my vulnerable condition, some friends installed a burglar alarm and outside lights. (Unfortunately, two anti-clerical, non-Catholic, night-clubbing cats keep setting them all off from midnight on.) But however long the night, the morning always comes. Once again, with daylight, everything seems normal and safe.

Anyway, I am now convinced that the only way to beat the fear in our lives, is to face it. You cannot escape it, or outrun it. You can only meet it, confront it, and then what usually happens is, the fear just evaporates. The monster you are fleeing from does not exist – except in your own imagination. Very often our fear has its roots in childhood. Do you remember the dark at the top of the stairs?

As a priest, I hear confessions and many trust me with their secrets. I am, as a consequence, very aware of the power of fear and anxiety in people's lives. Fear cripples our creativity, it diminishes our joys, it makes us suspicious of others, it makes us doubt ourselves. Fear drains the colour from our days, the dreams from our nights.

Susan Jeffers wrote a book called *Feel the fear and do it anyway*! It is about realising what happens when fear controls our lives. Jeffers helps us to see that while fear can clearly diminish and even destroy our joy and freedom, it can also be a hidden grace. It is only when we are afraid – at the moment of our fear – that we can take a unique step forward into a new, personal freedom, into another stage of growing towards God. Confronting fear in this way takes courage.

Our fear draws attention to those parts of our lives that are unprotected, underdeveloped and undernourished. Why, for instance, do I worry so much about what might happen to my children? Why am I afraid of what the neighbours might be saying about me? Why am I terrified of not being 'good enough' to please my boss, to hold on to my partner, to avoid failure in my life? As I grow older, why do I fear becoming unattractive, becoming more dependent and more isolated?

These are life-giving questions. If we spend our 15 minutes each day reflecting on them, we will find a new motivation and energy. We will stop living our lives to please others, trying to be successful all the time, unable to grow older gracefully. For the first time in our lives, maybe, we will begin to live freely as our authentic selves. It is only then that God becomes the centre of our existence.

Jacket or strait-jacket?
Many of us never find our true shape

When it comes to buying a suit, I'm an off-the-peg kind of customer. I'm neither a big man nor a small man – I'm somewhere in the middle. I was recently trying on a suit-jacket, in a local store, in preparation for a North Yorkshire winter. I was feeling pressurised by the sales attendant to purchase a suit that I did not feel comfortable in – something that wasn't really 'me'. I resisted the pressure and decided to wait for another day – and another store! As I left the place, a story came to mind. It's about how we often live our lives to suit other people.

A young man came to collect a suit his tailor had made for him. When he tried it on he noticed that one side was longer than the other. When he pointed this out to the tailor he was told that his suit would be a perfect fit if he held one shoulder higher than the other. The young man also noticed that one leg of the trousers was too long. When he pointed this out, the tailor told him that the suit would look great if he held his arm at an angle and if he walked with a limp. The tailor was so persuasive that the young man decided to wear the new suit on his way home, confident that it would create the impression he wanted to create. As he was walking through the park, two old men sitting on a bench noticed him. One on them commented with sympathy on how crippled the young man was, but the other said, 'Ah yes, but what a suit!'

We often twist ourselves out of shape just to conform to the demands of fashion, of looking good, of being 'cool' and 'with it'. More seriously, perhaps, we also twist our lives out of shape so as to be accepted by others, to meet their expectations, to make a good impression. So much of our energy goes into the externals of each day and to the superficial aspects of living.

We miss the deeper dimensions of the gift of our lives. Our hearts and souls often remain dangerously undernourished. We are so busy living on the surface of things that we forget about the more abundant life deeper down – that place where so much of our potential, so many of our gifts and powers, remain untouched.

Do you remember the film *Shirley Valentine*? Shirley grows increasingly aware of how confined her life has become. She has allowed herself to become a slave of the expectations of others and, as a result, she has left much of her dream unrealised. 'I've led such a little life,' she said, 'and even that will be over pretty soon. I've allowed myself to lead this little life when inside me there is so much more and it's all gone unused. And now it will never be.'

May all of us truly *live* our lives and our dreams at the deepest levels.

Collecting on the streets
Don't take it personally!

It was a rainy Saturday morning in the Market Place. Having asked others to collect money for our local Cancer Hospice on that October day, I felt it only right that I should do so myself as well. My 'patch' was between the Post Office and the Wine Rack. I did not find it an easy task.

Every time I rattled the can and asked for a contribution, I had to take a deep breath. Every time I forced myself to catch someone's eye, hoping they would smile and stop, I had to say a silent prayer of hope. How I longed for friendly faces, for people to recognise either the St Gemma's Hospice sticker or myself.

I found it quite hard to ask for help. It brought out my fear of appearing needy and inadequate. I much prefer to be the strong one, the one who gives, who has 'got it all together', who is successful and complete. I find it so difficult to say 'Please help me; I'm struggling. I'm not as self-sufficient as you think I am.' I'm happier, I have learned, when I'm in control.

During those few wet hours I learned much about myself – about my embarrassed pride and lack of humility, about my quickness to judge those people who passed me by without a glance or a penny, about how good I felt to be parading my virtues in front of others, about my fear of being rejected by the busy shoppers and therefore, at the end of the day, would my tin be the lightest of them all? In short, what came home to me was a renewed sense of my vulnerability and fragility. For a man, and for a preacher-man at that, such a realisation is a difficult pill to swallow.

Don't judge anybody we are told, until you have walked a few miles in their moccasins. I have a new respect and compassion now, for all those we meet each week in our towns and cities, collecting revenue for good causes, offering raffle-tickets for community amenities, or selling *The Big Issue*. Some of these collector-people have told me about the abuse they receive from our unhappy humans. But, they said, they have learned not to take it personally.

There is a lesson here for all of us. 'Don't take it personally'.

So many of the tantrums we throw, the childish pouts and silences we inflict on others, are all due to the fact that our vanity or pride is punctured because we take things personally, when, in fact, we really should not bother. Those careless comments usually spring from the other person's distress and we, at the receiving end, are very foolish to take them personally.

Most of us carry a great insecurity inside us. That is what makes us so sensitive to criticism, real or imagined. Those with a healthy self-esteem seem able to shrug off the negative remarks and gestures with greater ease than those of us who allow them to fester too long in our minds and hearts. How often do we eventually come to realise that the impact of the perceived insult arose, not from someone else's malice, but from our own fear. Gradually we learn to see things more objectively – not to take it personally.

In spite of everything, however, it was a great experience to be out there collecting. People were wonderful – both my many colleagues who do this kind of thing quietly and regularly, and also, the citizens of our cities who open their purses and wallets, with a humorous remark, and maybe not even knowing who benefits from their generosity.

God goes to infants' class
Even Jesus had to be potty-trained

I called in to the Reception Class of our Primary School recently. Jill, their teacher, was utterly concentrating on her numeracy work with the little ones. Each child, in turn, was walking on some mats numbered 1, 2, 3, 4, etc. 'Call out the numbers as you walk,' she would gently ask them. 'Now Elizabeth, what comes after 4?'

I reflected afterwards, with Jill, about similar moments in the lives of, say, Albert Einstein and Stephen Hawkins. We find it hard to believe that the geniuses of our universe once had to learn the most elementary facts. There was a time, for instance, when someone once said to Shakespeare, 'This is how you make an A,' and 'Well done, William, now make a B.'

There was also a time when someone said to Mozart, 'No Amadeus, try again. It is not doh-me-re; it is doh-re-me. The 're' comes after the 'doh'.' Or again, did someone once have to say to Michelangelo, 'Look Michael, that colour is green, not yellow.'

I find this kind of reflection both enjoyable and enriching. But what is most extraordinary and almost unbelievable is that, once upon a time, even God, too, like the rest of us, had to learn to walk, talk, dress, write, paint and dance. To understand something of the mystery of the incarnation, we must brace ourselves for a tremendous shock: that in the baby Jesus, God took on *all* the limitations and growth-stages of every baby. The best of our Christian tradition insists that God was as truly present and incarnate in every stage of the infancy and childhood of Jesus, as that same God was in the fullness of the life, death and resurrection of the miracle-working, transfigured and crucified Christ.

Part of us does not want to accept this. It just cannot be true. How could the God of all creation become so fragile, so vulnerable, so ordinary? God in a tiny baby! But that is what love does. Love surrenders itself and becomes powerless. All of this takes our breath away. While other religions have their own marvellous accounts of God's ways of being with us, the Christian incarnation story has a human reality that stops us in our tracks.

I don't want to get too heavy or too demanding in this reflection, but there is one more wisdom-step for you to take – one
that may bless you for the rest of your life. It is about the simple
but profound truth that because God once became human in a
small child called Jesus, God is now intimately present in every
child. Many of you know this already in your hearts. Since the
first Christmas, when a vulnerable baby revealed the fullness of
God's love, we now know that every baby is already shining
with God, and one day, with love, will become exactly like God.
And the same is true for you and for me. Do you really, really
believe this?

On that morning with Jill and the children, the celebrated
words of Pablo Casals, the famous cellist, came to mind: 'Do you
know what you are? You are a marvel. You are unique. In all the
world there is no other child exactly like you. And look at your
body – what a wonder it is. Your legs, your arms, your cunning
fingers, the way you move. You may become a Shakespeare, a
Michelangelo, a Beethoven. You have the capacity for anything.'

The ultimate challenge
When the last crutch is removed

I have a recurring nightmare. I open the morning paper to find my name and photo splashed across the front page. The news is bad about Daniel O'Leary. I'm now in disgrace. How can I face my people at the Sunday morning Mass? What will they say? Is this the end? And where can I hide?

The late Cardinal Bernardin of Chicago was a great and humble prophet of Love. He had two deadly fears in his life – the fear of disgrace and the fear of cancer. After mid-life, they both struck. He spent twelve months of pure pain when he was falsely accused of criminal behaviour before he was finally acquitted. His cancer was then discovered and he soon died. But during his final few months, having faced the two great fears of his life, he walked tall, his friends said, elegant and graceful, a free man.

There is a deep desire in all of us is to be truly ourselves. But to be truly ourselves means to stop relying on something outside ourselves for our happiness. The more I try to face life without this crutch or that, the more powerful I become. It takes courage to face the void that waits when we strip ourselves of unnecessary needs – things and people we thought essential for our lives to be complete.

We grow into our true selves, not by adding more to them, but by letting go of much that we accumulate in the course of our lives – in particular what we become too dependent on. There is no end to the list of all that over-attracts and seduces us. We become addicted so easily – to status, to power, to being-in-control, to substances, to titles, to habits of posturing, posing and preening, to popularity and to people. To be free we need to be sprung from such traps. But, strange as it seems, we are, so often, afraid to be free. We cannot face our naked selves. We need all kinds of support-systems to keep us believing in our worth and value.

When I was small my parents kept instilling in me the necessity of having a good reputation, of always keeping my good name. As long as I had that, they said, I had everything. Now I'm not so sure. We can become dependent too on being hailed as the foremost citizen, the high-priest. That too is a seductive kind of prison – one from which we need to be released if we are ever to become our own authentic selves, to travel light, to be free at last.

How many times, for instance, did Jesus, in his humanity, face the same challenging questions? How much he must have struggled in the desert with the demons of prestige, privilege and power. What a dying it was for him to let go of all of that. And how often did his good name lay in smithereens around him? So as to empty himself completely, he, too, had to make the choice between the clerical structures he inherited and the vision of God he carried in his heart, between his tempted ego and his authentic essence.

In the end, it all makes you wonder whether those shattering moments of public humiliation are necessary for certain souls. Maybe God reserves these ultimate challenges for special friends. Maybe such disgrace is the final grace – the last block to be removed, the last crutch to be kicked away, before we place our trust completely in the jealous heart of our human-God.

'He'll be here by midnight'
Your inner child is still alive: but is she well?

Michael Crawford and Cilla Black were on TV with Michael Parkinson recently. They spoke a lot about their childhood. It is almost impossible, they said, to underestimate the influence of our early experiences on our adult lives today. While many of us feel sure that we were happy as children, it often turns out that this is not the full story. Very few of us escape our childhood unscathed.

We are all victims of one kind of abuse or another. There is physical abuse by certain kinds of parents; there is also emotional abuse and even spiritual abuse by the priests, teachers and many others in our young years. That is why almost all of us carry some kind of wounded child within us.

What Michael Crawford was saying on the box, last week, was that unless we start to listen to the voice of that forgotten and forlorn child within us, we will never truly live. We will be trapped, at best, into a life of routine and mediocrity, and, at worst, into an existence of depression and cynicism about everything.

There are moments in our troubled lives when we are forced to stop and listen because our inner, wounded child is crying for attention; when the child we ignored because something else seemed more attractive at the time, begs of us not to leave her; when the child who simply wanted to laugh and play was given no more room to do so.

People are searching all over the place, these days, for inner happiness, for inner peace. Most 'self-help' programmes and books encourage us to revisit the wounds of our childhood. Our inner wounded child searches for spiritual nourishment. She yearns for a God of gentle understanding and of tender compassion. For Catholics, especially, (and for others, too, I'm sure) our childhood wounds have much to do with a God of vengeance and punishment.

Much of this strange pain has to do with the fact that our parents were not perfect. They, too, were struggling with their own childhood experiences. They, too, were victims of their own environment. They, too, were convinced of their righteousness when they did the best they could to mould and fix us into the shape they thought was the best for our future. Our childhood, then, carries memories that bless and burn. They have a magic and a mystery that can destroy or save us.

I still remember a Christmas Eve when I was four. The snow had begun to fall. I was beside myself with excitement about the imminent arrival of Santa Claus. I was standing near the small door that divided our small shop from our small kitchen. It was about 9.30 pm. Christy Cremin, a neighbour, had just bought his weekly packet of Woodbines. 'Where is he now, Christy?' my mother called out. I shivered with excitement. 'Oh, he's down beyond at the crossroads. I've just seen him there.' he replied. 'He'll be here by midnight.'

Why is my heart weeping as I write these words?

God with skin on
Our guardian angels can really touch us

On Tuesday morning I was blessing the Advent wreath at our school assembly. The Headmaster had explained the meaning of the four coloured candles, one to be lit each week before Christmas. 'What is most important of all,' he stressed, 'is that our hearts, too, should shine out for each other. We should all be candles of love for those around us.'

Now it so happened that I was a little depressed that morning. After many draining demands, the prospect of another long day's work was getting me down. Having said the blessing, I was sitting among the gathered parents. I had my head in my hands, my shoulders hunched. For some reason I looked up. Right in front of me, tiny as a tot, her arms stretched as wide as the sky, stood a smiling three-year-old. 'Fr Daniel,' she whispered, 'can I give you a hug?' I swear I will carry that memory to my grave. It was a glimpse of pure, spontaneous grace. I had not known Rachel before. Her teacher, Catherine, had not urged her on. On a dark and cold December morning, Rachel, like an Advent candle, brought light and warmth into my worried heart.

I'm reflecting, this evening, on that special moment. I realise that this is the only way that God can reach us, touch us, console us. Since the first Christmas, God is forever committed to healing and holding us through each other. That is the real magic of this season – the essential reason for all the celebrating we do. The incarnation of God means that our deep need for being comforted can now only come in a human way. We can scarcely believe how intimately God is present to us – in every word, smile and tear.

There is a story about the fearful child who, during the night, called out for his mother. She came into his room and spoke to him about the protection of the angels and of God all around him. He refused to be satisfied by her reassurances. 'I want something with skin on!' he blurted out. And that is what God does in becoming human at Christmas.

People like Rachel are the real angels. Do you ever notice how often angels come into your life? It is God's way of using us to heal and console each other. When I become aware of those hidden surprises in my life, it is as if Someone who loves me intensely, who follows every move I make all day long, is trying every way to keep me from suffering more pain than I can bear.

'So what's the big deal?' you might ask. 'Coincidences like that just happen.' And maybe you're right. Maybe I am getting carried away. Maybe it is all mere happen-chance. Maybe there is no loving Presence out there, desperately seeking ways and means to tenderly hold us, to dry our tears, to hug us and to kiss away our pain like mothers and lovers do.

Let me return to Rachel. Next year Rachel will be four. I dedicate these two final verses of Christopher Morley's poem about childhood to her, by way of honouring her divinity:

The greatest poem ever known
Is one all poets have outgrown:
The poetry, innate, untold,
Of being only four years old.

And Life, that sets all things in rhyme,
May make you poet, too, in time –
But there were days, O tender elf,
When you were poetry itself!

Salvation as symphony
When the Noise becomes the Music

The perennial *Glenn Miller Story* was on TV last Sunday afternoon. Here was a man looking for a certain sound in his orchestra. He carried the texture and feeling of it in his heart, but could not get it together in any combination of instruments and vocalists. One day it happened. When we listen to 'In the Mood' or 'String of Pearls' we experience the emotion he wished to evoke in us – our profound reaction to that rich, unique blend of magic he created.

This kind of reflecting helps me to understand better the long lead-up to, and the meaning of Christmas. Imagine you are in a concert-hall before the concert begins. It is a confused, unsure kind of atmosphere. There is much shuffling around as people look for their places. The orchestra, too, is tuning up in a discordant kind of way. Each instrument is doing its own thing and nothing seems to flow. But even in the confusion, there is an expectancy that all will come right; a hint, a promise of something joyful very soon.

It is as though all the noises and interruptions were searching for a lost melody – waiting for the clear theme of the symphony to emerge. At exactly the right moment, on comes the conductor who carries the full creation of the composer in his head and heart, who places the open score on the podium, who taps the baton, and calls for silence. And then, breathtakingly, something truly beautiful begins to unfold.

Maybe it was a little like that before the first Christmas night. There was a waiting world, full of vague hopes and flying rumours. The music of creation, the plan and plot for the universe, and everyone in it, had been lost or forgotten. Yet now there was a buzz of hope, a sense of expectancy. But who would it be – the one to put it all together? Who had the final picture of the various jig-saw pieces strewn across the table of the world? Who would take the torn tapestry of God's initial creation and restore it to its original beauty? Who would bring clarity to the chaos, meaning to the confusion, light to those in darkness, and music to the broken chords?

It was the baby. It was the baby who changed the history and destiny of the world by uniting, in his own tiny frame, the humanity of us and the divinity of God. It was the baby who, in his frail self, *was* the music, the song, the smile of a delighted God. His small heart *was* true North. It was the symphony of the baby's own self that the world played that first holy night at God's proms. And what was revealed, forever, in the final crescendo, was the unbelievable truth that the mighty majesty of God is most perfectly portrayed in the small cry, the slightly puzzled face and the fragile body of a new-born baby! This is the infusion of pure love that our world needs now.

There is one more thing to be said here, another dimension to be considered. There will always be something paradoxical about the vision of Jesus and about its realisation on earth. All the music is written but not all of it has been played. In spite of the images we have just been creating, we have here no finished symphony. Yes, Jesus *is* the complete score – lyrics and music. But we, extending into time and space, are now the heart of it. That is why, here, the pages have to keep turning. The melody will never end on this earth. Nobody can put this part of the mystery better than Karl Rahner: in the torment of the insufficiency of everything attainable we eventually realise that, here in this life, all symphonies remain unfinished.

In the meantime, even though we won't be around for the final crescendo, we owe it to each other to stay in tune.

In praise of space
We need reminders of another way of living

I find space very beautiful. In our recently designed new church in Leeds, we kept the huge back wall behind the altar completely empty. (But people are always trying to fill it with something or other!) Late at night, if the sky is cloudy, I search for any football match on TV, just for the restful healing of watching green space. How strange it is that people see space as waste.

Here in my current parish, I love the newly created space between the huge, landmark obelisk and the Town Hall in our Market Place. (But every so often there are those who want to turn it into a taxi-rank, a parking lot or a mobile shopping area!) This blessing has been a long time in coming. When I walk across it, I pray that all who do so will create within their hearts an inner space, as well, for all to grow. You might call it 'Soul-Space'. There seems to be a conspiracy against free space. Emptiness is seen as loss, as missed opportunity. Every square inch of everything must be used for something. But in their wisdom our city planners were ready to see emptiness, not as threat but rather as gift.

We forget to appreciate the value of space and of spaces. Without the blank margins on the page before you just now, you could not read it. If ever we are to hear a story or a song, there has to be spaces between the letters of a word, silence between the notes of a melody. It is important to think about these things. Just walking across any new space, especially in busy places, makes me slow down. It makes me ask myself how I'm doing today, why I'm rushing so much, why I don't stop and breathe more slowly and just look around me? Soon enough I'll be dead; then I'll be sorry I missed so much of my one, beautiful life.

I have been called to many a deathbed to pray for the dying, but never yet have I heard anyone say, 'I wish I had spent more time washing up, or more time at the office!' What people *do* express on their deathbeds is the regret they carry for not spending more time at play with their partners, children or grandchildren, for more hours spent in fooling around and wasting time with them, for not sitting in some Market Place with gloves and scarf on a snowy evening, or with an ice-cream and long memories on a summer's day.

Citizens here were asked for suggestions about activities for the new Market Place space so as 'to bring a smile back to our small city'. But the smile I long to see is the smile of the tired and hassled young mother, with two or three crying young children in tow, as she sits down in the traffic-free safety of the new space and kicks off her shoes for one brief life-giving moment. Or the frazzled young shop-assistant as he grabs a sandwich, and pauses there, during his twenty-minute lunch-break. Or a middle-aged couple who, on a quiet evening, sit and say to each other, 'Well, that family of ours, they're not doing so badly, are they? Maybe, after all, we haven't done so bad a job!'

It is so important to keep such a hard-won space free of all structures. People will forever try to fill it – there is always the human tendency to clutter things up. But here we have a pearl of great price. We need to protect it. At the heart of how many cities can children chase each other around in safety? Or where, in the relentless hustle-bustle of most thronged centres, can one pause in the open air, to silently whisper a brief prayer of desperation or of gratitude to the Mystery of Life? Or, under God's safe sky, where else can we dream our personal dreams in the sun, or search for our star on a warm night? That's what space is for.

Time to smell the roses
Celebrating the sacrament of the present moment

Do you remember the poem from school, 'What is life if, full of care, We have no time to stand and stare'? I'm convinced that one of the secrets of an interesting and satisfying life is to notice things, to be attentive to what is going on around you, not to miss the moment of what is happening, to spot the hidden details of things.

Did you, for instance, notice how full, round and yellow the moon has been recently? How bright the stars? Have you felt a whisper of Spring in the breeze these last few days, in spite of the rain and changeable weather? To be aware of such things brings much healing. It is a natural kind of way for de-stressing ourselves. Sitting in the Spa Gardens and noticing all the teeming life among the blades of grass and weeds gently takes our minds off ourselves and provides a breathing space for our troubled souls.

So often we miss these pleasures of the senses. Do we ever stay still for a moment to savour the lovely pink dawns of these February/March days, to feel the different textures of our skin or that of another, to taste the wet spurt of the apple in our mouth when we crunch it, to sense the feeling in our body on the first really warm day of Spring or, just in time, to notice the beauty of the small cobweb we were just going to destroy?

What we fail to notice is usually right in front of us. Have you ever dwelt, with a kind of reverence, on the miracle of the human body – your own and others – when you run up or down the stairs after your children, when you hold the one you love closely, when you taste the rain on your tongue, when you feel the strength returning to your limbs after an illness, when you relax in a hot bath after a trying day?

For instance, the colour and texture of the fields in North Yorkshire are now changing by the day. There are ripening flowers and trees on the streets where we live. People talk about a new spirit in our city, a new spring in the steps of its citizens. What a source of reflection the weekly market is, as people come to sell what they have made or grown in their farms, and others buy them to bring home for their family. And all the while there is conversation and community-making. I sometimes think that the history of humanity is re-enacted in the barter and banter of every Thursday Market.

Last week I locked myself out of the Parish House. You can imagine my panic. I had two hours of broken appointments to sweat out. Deliberately trying to follow my own advice about dropping my shoulders and relaxing my face, I walked to the Market Place and sat down in the calm new space we have created there. I tried to let go of my anxiety. Taking a few deep breaths, I said to myself: 'Oh, what the heck! Its not the end of the world.' I looked up at the ancient obelisk in the centre of the square, shining like a mighty needle against a threadbare sky. What secrets it must be carrying, I thought, having watched over our streets for more than three centuries! And what a life it had long before it arrived in Europe. How many were watching, I wondered, on that day in 1702, when the local mason, high and important, tapped his trowel against the very last pointed stone and proudly placed that golden horn, the emblem of our city, at the top? Did the crowd shout and clap? How were the people dressed? Did they dance, and to what kind of music? Did their spirits lift with the soaring obilisk?

Then suddenly, like the angel who appeared to St Paul in prison, along came Roni with a spare key!

The power of saying 'I love you'
Don't put it off any longer

Sometimes I get a card that says 'I love you.' It is always a shock when someone writes or says those most special words. Sometimes they are said between friends and relations in a beautifully meaningful way. Whereas I never said 'I love you' to my father before he died, I said it repeatedly to my mother during the last precious years of our time together.

It is so important to tell people that we love them, even though we may find it very difficult to do so. Some find it embarrassing. Others were told it might lead them into trouble. Men may feel it is wimpish. Whatever the reason, we often leave it too late. Someone close to us dies and, for a long time, we regret not having assured them of our love. Will we ever forget the desperate mobile messages of aching intimacy from those aboard that doomed plane on 11 September?

Because we are made by God to love and to be loved, our lives will be always unfulfilled until we nourish that hunger within us. 'If you give your heart to no one,' wrote C. S. Lewis, 'it will become unbreakable, impenetrable and irredeemable.' Our hearts are made to be given away. Like the heart of Jesus, they are sacred in their human loving. 'The love with which we love each other,' wrote St Augustine, 'is the same love with which God loves us.' The Christian Church was founded on the human friendship and love of Jesus for the women and men around him.

When we tell people we love them truly, we redeem them with God's life. Instead of possessing them, we set them free. At our pre-marriage talks, I try to point out to couples the difference between total fusion and a certain independence in their mutual commitment. There are those who give over all their power to the partner and, with it, often their self-esteem too. It is possible to diminish oneself (and the other) by becoming too dependent. That is not true love; maybe more like addiction. Gibran puts it very well in *The Prophet*:
Love one another, but make not a bond of love:
Let it rather be a moving sea between the shores of your souls.

81

Sing and dance together and be joyous, but let each of you be alone,
Even as the strings of the lute are alone though they quiver with the
same music. And stand together, yet not too near together:
For the pillars of the temple stand apart,
And the oak tree and the cypress grow not in each other's shadow.

I am very aware of the power of those words 'I love you'.
They can change our lives for ever. When said from the heart,
there are no more transforming moments. I think God needs us
to whisper these words to each other. God is love and wherever
love is, God is. And some suffering too! 'If you dare to love, be
prepared to grieve.'

Are there those who never heard such words? Or people
who never said them? And is there still time? In spite of the tears
that come with love, could this be the pearl of great price that
lies hidden in one of the summer fields along your life's path
this year?

Is my child safe?
Our children are an endangered species

Whenever I feel stressed out I think of youngish parents and the way they manage to cope with so many challenges to their time, energy and mental stability. Many of them find it very difficult. The pressure of work and family on mothers is often costly in terms of strain and damage to health – mental and physical. Tiredness, frayed nerves, keeping up appearances – so many are close to breaking point.

On top of that are the signs that all is not well with the general health of children either – victims, too, of the relentless dis-ease of frantic family life. This very week, some rather worrying facts are emerging about the mental health of children. We have known for some time that eight-year-olds can suffer from depression. Now it is being revealed that much younger children can be affected. The head of child psychology services for a NHS trust identified clinical depression as widespread among the very young in our society.

Recent research by London's City University found alarmingly high levels of stress among children under ten. Karen Sullivan, author of *Kids Under Pressure*, holds that the psychological damage caused to children by such stress is immeasurable. Very often it is the unfinished business of the parents that piles the pressure on their children. The expectations of many parents are too high.

The author believes that parents over-schedule the lives of their children, enrolling them in too many activities such as language courses, computer courses and music lessons. Like so many driven adults, children, too, are expected to be usefully busy all the time, thus depriving them of vital opportunities to mess about, to play, to hang around or maybe just to do nothing.

A few years ago I was 'official starter' at a school sports day. At the end of a race I overheard a tearful seven-year-old, who came in second, explain to his father that he had 'done his best'. 'Well, son,' the angry Dad replied, 'your best wasn't good enough, was it? You'll have to do better, won't you?'

Even though reports may be exaggerated, my heart goes out

to parents these days, at the numerous reports of the growing incidence of obesity, asthma and hyperactivity among small children. I sound like a real pessimist this week! Thankfully, the majority of children will never experience stress or depression, or any of the other listed ailments, in their childhood, and, hopefully, throughout their lives. But all children are precious and, especially at a time of ruthless manipulation, it is better to risk overstating the case, rather than, self-indulgently, to ignore the warning signs.

It is disturbing to discover some of the adult symptoms of stressful living in those so small. How do we protect such vulnerable, defenceless lives from our grown-up foolish ways? God's face shines out from young faces. When our children are not well, the colour and health drains from all our bodies and souls. May our little ones be always held safely by their guardian angels.

The first blessing
God is incarnate from the start, in a mother's love

My life wears many colours and has taken endless twists and turns. The decades of my earthly journey have carried all kinds of lights and shadows, virtues and vices, blessings and burdens. But through it all there has been one shining conviction forever holding me together – the certainty that I am well loved. Time and again, when all other supports have collapsed, and the temptation to despair is very strong, this fierce belief that I somehow matter a great deal, fills me with new and powerful resolve.

With all my heart I know that it was the love of my mother that gifted me with that flaming centre, to light my way when many other loves failed. My childhood must have filled me with a sense that my mother was delighted with me, that she was proud of me, that I was a wholesome person. It was through her, I believe, that I felt good about myself, felt that I was worthy of respect, enabling me to be secure enough to take the risks in life that I am called to take.

Without this inner experience of being unconditionally loved, how else could I understand that I am so extravagantly loved by God? So many otherwise fine souls feel so bad about themselves – too unworthy, too unattractive to be loved by God. Maybe there was nobody in their lives, during their childhood, to assure them that they were the apple of someone's eye, that they were precious to another.

What a divine responsibility for any mother – to be the one who opens a child up, or closes her down, to the beautiful love of a beautiful God. There is something about the compassionate devotion of God that can only be captured on this earth by the selfless and unique heart of a mother. The total and unconditional love with which a mother holds her fretting baby, strokes her child's hair, wraps her in a towel after her bath, wakes up every night to comfort and soothe the troubled dreams of her toddler, overlooks yet another sudden tantrum – these moments and a million more are the truest reflection in our young lives of the constant love of our Mother-God for all of us.

It is the mother's smile, her touch, her voice that awakens love in the heart of the little one. The child is coaxed and cajoled into an awareness of beckoning life by the eyes and whispers of the mother. The small baby is caressed and lured outside herself, into delighted, kicking self-expression, by the playful fingers and words of the devoted mother. Maybe most of all, the tiny heart is opened to its first pang of compassion when, for whatever reason, it feels the mysterious tears of its adored companion. And all of this is God's work too. As the gentle morning sun persuades the daisy to open its eyes, it is the light of God, in mother and baby, that creates this miraculous awakening. How else could God enjoy the sensation of holding, enticing and celebrating the most wonderful miracle of new life, if not through mothers?

As we celebrate Mothers' Day this weekend, my wish to you, the mothers of our community, is that your children may one day bless and honour you, as I do my mother, for the fire of inner conviction she lit in my heart. One evening, using my Irish name, my mother left this Celtic blessing on my pillow:

> *Be thine the encompassing of the God of life;*
> *Be thine the encompassing of the Christ of love;*
> *Be thine the encompassing of the Spirit of grace,*
> *To befriend thee and to aid thee,*
> *O Donal, beloved of my breast:*
> *to befriend thee and to aid thee,*
> *thou beloved of my heart.*

The mystery of the cross
If you dare to love, be prepared to grieve

There is one occasion in the year when we gather to watch the figure of a man on a cross, outlined starkly against a fading light, and there is always a thoughtful child who asks the perennial question 'Why do we call Good Friday "good"?' It is a profound question. Another way of putting it is, 'If Jesus was a man of love, why was he killed? And if this good man was killed, why do we celebrate it? Why do love and pain go together?'

In his famous book *The Prophet*, Kahlil Gibran writes: 'Some of you say that love and joy are greater than sorrow, and others say, "Nay, sorrow is the greater.' But I say unto you, they are inseparable. Together they come, and when one sits alone with you at your table, remember that the other is asleep upon your bed.'

The shell must break before the chicken walks free; the seeds must die before we celebrate the harvest. Elgar, the composer, once said of a student, 'She is an excellent singer. But she will not be a great one until she suffers more.' There is no other way. Seen through the lens of the Christian Easter mystery, our suffering becomes our friend, our pain opens our hearts to compassion. If we take up our cross, as Jesus asks us to, our cross will be our salvation; it will prune and purify us; it will lead us safely home.

Once upon a time there was a man who had a cross to carry through life. It was a particularly awkward and cumbersome cross and he complained much about it. Journeying through the valley, he met another man who felt sorry for him and suggested that if he sawed a bit off the bottom of the cross it would be much lighter to carry. Delighted with the good advice, the man cut off a piece from the bottom and, much lighter, continued on his way. Some years later, as he neared the city at the end of his travels, he came to a river. He looked in vain for a bridge. The only way across from one bank to the other, to reach the City of Joy, was to lay the cross down as a bridge and clamber over. Laying the base of the cross on the near bank, he lowered the cross so that the tip of it might touch the far bank. But the cross was too short – by about the length sawn off.

There is another reason for calling Good Friday 'good'. It reveals to us for ever what love is prepared to do. Many of us are familiar with an incident recorded by the Jewish writer Eli Wiesel. In one of the Nazi death camps, a prisoner had escaped and, in retaliation, the Nazis took a young boy, hanged him publicly, and forced everyone to watch this horrific spectacle. As the young boy dangled on a rope in front of them, one man cursed bitterly: 'Where is God now?' Another answered: 'There, on that rope. That's God!'

One day I was called to the Intensive Care Unit of the Children's Ward. A baby had died. The broken-hearted parents were inconsolable and angry. 'Where is your God now?' they shouted at me. 'Holding you both and weeping with you,' I mumbled. It was then that he embraced her and gently said, 'You know I will always love you.' Some moments stay in your mind forever.

To a dancing God
Do you really believe the new song in your heart?

It is still Easter week. In one of the Western Isles of Scotland, over a hundred years ago, Barbara MacPhie of Dreimsdale recounted some of the ancient Celtic customs and ceremonies of Easter. Before dawn, she said, the whole parish would gather on a hilltop to wait, in the dark, for the rising of the sun over the timeless hills. She recalled one such Paschal Sunday morning when, before their very eyes, the golden ball of the early light began to dance in the sky in many circles of brilliant colour. 'It was dancing up and down,' she said, 'in pure joy before the Risen Son of God.'

With one part of our mind we dismiss this Gaelic piece of folklore as fanciful nonsense. Everyone knows that the sun does not dance. But another part of us wants to believe it. Maybe the sun did dance. Maybe the dance took place in her heart. And does it really matter where it happened? Easter is about a dancing Son of God, a new dance in our hearts and, maybe, a sun that dances in the sky.

Is your heart waiting to dance in you? In this more relaxed week after Easter we have a chance to reflect on that part of us that wants to play and dance in the light. There is a childhood memory within us that wants to go barefoot in the summer, to dream in the autumn, to dance in the winter and to set seeds in the spring.

Each year I feel that Easter releases within us the amazing realisation that we want to play, to be free, to be truly ourselves. Easter is about letting go of our fear, of our half-life, of our over-seriousness. Easter is not about some airy-fairy, pie-in-the-sky type of religion – about some quaint beliefs in a God that sentenced his Son to death. It is about the business of being truly human, truly ourselves, truly authentic in the very essence of our being.

The whole point of the Easter mystery is not to keep blaming ourselves for the awful crucifixion of Jesus. It is rather to rejoice that we are loved so much by God. 'The Greatest Story ever Told' is often twisted by religious spin-doctors. It is about God's compassion, not about God's anger. No matter what, we are always embraced by our 'Tremendous Lover'. Easter is the perennial reminder that, at whatever cost, love will always win. Death, divorce or despair will never have the last word. No amount of 11 Septembers will separate God from this beautiful world. When we believe all of these things, the sun, of course, dances a lovely dance in our hearts.

'I am the Spirit of the Risen Christ. If you dare to believe it, I can set free the dance in your body, the music in your soul, the adventure in your heart. You can overcome every fear – with me. You can forgive every hurt – with me. You can make your life a journey of wonder – with me. Every dream you carry inside you can come true – but only with me. You can mend your broken life, and this broken world, because now, everything is possible. You have, in fact, all my power for compassion at your disposal – you only have to claim it. Heaven on earth lies open before you today, for the taking. But there is one condition – you must dare to believe it.'

Letter to my son
The grace of a father's blessing

Some months ago a friend asked me to write down a few thoughts for his teenage son. If I had a son of my own, I would bless him like this:

Allow yourself to dream, to hold on to your childhood vision, and, however old you are, always try to follow that vision. And every time you lose it, because, in today's hard world, you will often forget it, then begin again and try to make that dream come true.

Give yourself permission to make mistakes. There is no other way to grow. Forgive yourself – easily and often. There are enough people out there who will condemn you. Until you begin to accept and even love your own weakness and vulnerability, you will never know the meaning of God's power and strength.

Allow yourself to have joy. The world can be a demanding place with relentless expectations. Some people feel guilty about loving themselves, about enjoying the pleasures of life. They grow very serious. Learn to laugh at yourself. Let your inner child come out to play, to be free, to wonder, to live in the present moment. That is why Jesus asked us to become like children.

Believe in your own ability, in your beauty, in the shining light of God that you carry. Many people are full of a strange self-hatred about their bodies and souls. Do not forget to be delighted with yourself, to be proud of who you are, to want to be nobody else. You are a little less than the angels; you are the glory of God, full of divine energy and healing. All of this you must believe.

Be nobody's victim. There are lots of people and systems out there trying to gain control over your heart and mind. There is enormous pressure on you and on your friends to conform your daily habits of eating, drinking, dressing and socialising to some unreal ideal dreamt up by profit-making and ruthless powers. So be careful about the people and the messages you follow; always remember to protect your heart.

In the professional work you choose, do what you love – the

money will follow. Channel your passion and creativity into your chosen career. Don't take the first job on offer. Your destiny will lead you; your angels will guide you. There are always other options.

Learn to accept the darkness and disappointments of your life. This is a slow and painful lesson. Without some form of suffering, you will never become compassionate. It is, in fact, impossible to be truly human, wise and joyful, without feeling your own pain and that of our beautiful, mutilated world. As Christians know, there can be no bright Easter morning without first a dark Good Friday.

Practise letting go of the mental baggage that can weigh you down. So much time is wasted in useless worry. Live in the present moment; it is the safest and most nourishing place to live.

I want you to believe, my son, in God's immense love for you. You will never walk alone. There is nothing to fear but fear itself. Always remember that. Let this truth be my blessing on you.

A time to laugh
On giving back to God the management of the world

The news is bad. As I listen to the awful stories about what is happening in the world, in our churches and in our cities, I find it very painful. Where and when will it end? We all feel somehow responsible for the suffering of others. These disturbing events drag us down. How do we best cope with the anxiety and worry?

Last week a few of us decided to go to the pictures in Warners Village in York. We parked in front of Frankie and Benny's Restaurant, where they play their music out on to the street. Dean Martin was belting out 'That's Amore'. (Remember it?) Instinctively two of us began to waltz around the road, much to the embarrassment of a group of well-behaved teenagers who quickly fled the scene. We laughed as the pent-up tension began to flow away. Our bodies and minds were beginning to feel better. (Did you know that literally hundreds of face-muscles relax with every smile?)

There is only so much bad news that we can take. The media pile it on, day after day. We struggle and pray for justice and peace at home and abroad, for an end to the massacres and abuse, for some signs and seeds of hope. But we cannot carry it all.

It is then that we hand it over, for the time being at least, to whatever God we believe in, to whatever Saviour has won our trust. We lighten up a little. We search for a new balance. Truly, we believe with Julian of Norwich, that all is well and that all manner of things will be well. Once we accept this wonderful good news, then the absent smile returns to our faces and the energy to our bodies. It does not mean that we forget about the plight of others; it is that we believe more strongly that a compassionate God has saved the world for now and always. It means that we accept and flow with this great mystery called Life that we cannot always understand.

It is then that we feel the spontaneous surge of life within us. It is then that we want to sing 'Alleluia' with the heavenly people or 'That's Amore' with a very earthly one. Our God is a God of exuberance and pleasure. Our God is the 'Lord of the Dance'.

Like any normal parent or true friend, nothing gives God more joy than to see us as happy as can be. It is easy for us to lose our spirit, to become negative about everything, to start criticising and blaming. A glance at the letter-pages in our newspapers will testify to that. God's chosen people can so quickly turn into God's frozen people.

In spite of everything, there are many deep reasons for happy hearts and dancing feet these weeks. We have celebrated Easter and we await the power of Pentecost. We have welcomed Spring and now we are on the cusp of Summer. Our city is looking good and the positive attitude of so many of our citizens is growing. And also, we count our own personal blessings too – every day. Then we know that this is God's way of saying 'You are always safe because I love you'. God does it better than old Deano!

Letter to my daughter
The grace of a mother's blessing

Having written a reflection that a father requested for his son, a mother asked me to write a blessing to give to her daughter. So here it is, for the teenage daughter I never had.

Let nobody own you. You are too precious to be possessed by anything or anyone. There will always be those around you who will try to make you feel small and inadequate. Only God is big enough for you. You are a child of the universe, fashioned from the stuff of the stars. Don't ever forget your divine heritage.

Learn to love yourself. That means loving those parts of you that others may criticise. Some women tend to think that they are not good enough – or they are made to feel that way. While you are still young, do not let those negative habits take root in your heart. Learn to be gentle and patient with yourself. Don't wait until later to love and trust yourself. Begin today.

Remember that the Power is within you. With God, there is nothing you cannot achieve. The only limits around us are the ones we ourselves draw! Without depending on substances or other people, you can take charge of your own life. The true voice within you will guide you safely through the necessary darkness.

Try to understand boys and men. Deep down they are in awe of women. They cover it over with all kinds of macho stuff. In fact I think many men are afraid of women! It may not be true in every instance. But it may help you at times to understand men's strange behaviour. Let no one disrespect you.

Be nobody's victim. There's something strange in many men that wants to victimise women. And there's something in many women that colludes with such behaviour. Do not let this happen to you. Let no one – man, government, church or family – ever take away your freedom. Make sure that your self-esteem is always high.

Don't be afraid to stand up for yourself. In religion, big business and politics, even now in the third millennium, the chips still seem to be stacked against you. But the balance is shifting.

There is a positive kind of feminism that is essential for young women today. You will often get it wrong. It is not weak to say 'I'm sorry.'

Know how to protect yourself. You have a mystery about you that must be carefully looked after. Do not let all your sails out to the wayward wind. Do not trust the wrong people with your magic cookies. May you always have the grace to discern the falsehood and lies in those who pretend that they love you.

Make sure you have a 'soul-friend'. This is a person who will never deceive you, flatter you or wish anything for you but your true happiness. Your soul-friend will listen to you, will weep and laugh with you, but will not be fooled by you. Like a wise guardian angel, your soul-friend will always walk with you, defend you and love you. You are the most important person in your life. And in mine.

Life-lines from the spirit
Taking lessons in humanity

During the Church's liturgical year, Christians continue to celebrate Lady Sophia, the Spirit of Wisdom, of Life, of God. In the course of my decades she has taught me many things. I have put together some of these 'Rules for being truly human'. All of those basic insights are hard to learn. Yet even one of them can change your life.

YOU WILL LEARN LESSONS: You are enrolled in a fulltime informal school called life. Each day in this school you will have the opportunity to learn lessons. You may like the lessons or you may not like them.

THERE ARE NO MISTAKES, ONLY LESSONS: Growth is a process of trial and error. The failures are as much part of the process as the successes.

A LESSON IS REPEATED UNTIL LEARNED: A lesson will be presented to you in various forms until you have learned it. The lessons that have not been learned will continue to reappear in your life.

LEARN TO LOVE YOUR BODY: You may not like it, but it will be yours for all of this lifetime. It is your best friend, the home you carry with you everywhere.

LEARNING LESSONS DOES NOT END: There is no part of life that does not contain lessons. If you are alive, there are lessons to be learned.

'THERE' IS NO BETTER THAN 'HERE': You will always want to be where you are not. You will always hanker after something you haven't got.

OFTEN TIMES, OTHERS ARE MIRRORS OF YOU: You cannot love or hate something about another person unless it reflects to you something you love or hate about yourself.

WHAT YOU MAKE OF YOUR LIFE IS UP TO YOU: You have all the tools and resources you need. What you do with them is up to you. The choice is yours.

YOUR ANSWERS LIE INSIDE OF YOU: The answers to life's questions lie inside you. All you need to do is look, listen and trust your inner voice.

WATCH YOUR WISHES: Whatever you wish for others will one day appear in your own life. This applies to the negative things as well as to the positive.

YOU WILL FIND LIFE HARD: Don't waste time trying to make it easy for yourself. For some strange reason we expect to he happy all the time.

YOU WILL CERTAINLY DIE: Never forget how precarious and unpredictable your life is. It is only when you accept this truth that you can live freely.

YOU ARE NOT THAT IMPORTANT: Do not forget how insignificant you are in the grand scheme of things, in the vast mysteries of time and space.

YOU ARE NOT IN CONTROL OF YOUR LIFE: This is one of the hard lessons to learn. It is about humility and everyone has to taste it. Ultimately, we are all fairly powerless.

YOUR LIFE IS NOT ABOUT YOU: You are about life! Your place is on your knees – to wonder, to adore, to be thankful and to serve. When you exploit and manipulate others you only diminish yourself. Your one, wild and precious life is about respect, not greed.

YOU ARE A CHILD OF THE UNIVERSE: Live your life in that awareness. There is nothing that is not a part of you. Tread on a daisy and trouble a star.

YOU HAVE ACCESS TO LIMITLESS POWER: If you want to believe it, and if you open yourself to the Higher Power, there is nothing that you cannot do or be. The healing wisdom within you will be awakened; you will be empowered to be free.

The dreamer within
Wake up to your dreams' wisdom

A kitten and a snake were playing with each other. I watched them with great apprehension. I felt that something terrible would happen at any moment. I then, calmly and clinically, cut out a neat section of someone's head. There was only a slight smear of blood on the shining blade. (Are you still reading this?) I'm referring to my most recent remembered dream. I still have no idea what it means. I will work on it with some friends as soon as I can.

We all dream. Some people remember their dreams. Occasionally, our dreams can be of great benefit in our searching for the way ahead and for guidance here and now. All our dreams are there to help and heal us. That is why every dream is a gift. Even those frightening dreams we call nightmares – they call our attention to some unhealthy aspect of our lives by scaring us so we will not forget!

The meanings of our dreams are never obvious. If they were, they would not bother to come to us in the first place. They are very subtle, creative and often humorous. They have several layers of meaning. Sometimes they come in colour; sometimes in black and white. Most of the characters in every dream represent an aspect of ourselves.

It is important to be sympathetic and not cynical about our dreams. They respond to invitation. Before you sleep, ask your unconscious to visit you that night. Be open to its arrival. In preparation it is advised to have a pen and paper by the side of your bed. It is almost impossible to remember a dream later on in the day. Write them down in the present tense and give them titles. Express them in any manner you wish – poetry, drawings, even a bit of a dance. Play around with them. Ask them back. They are on your side!

For Sigmund Freud, dreams were 'the royal road to the unconscious' and therefore of unimaginable therapeutic value for our psychic well-being. Some counsellors and therapists pay particular attention to the dreams of their clients. In spiritual direction, too, it is often claimed that God whispers to us in our dreams. There is much evidence of this in the Bible.

When 'working with a dream', try to notice the pattern of your dreams. Look at your whole life in a relaxed way. Pay attention to any aspect of the dream that sticks out in your memory. This may only be a fragment, a colour, a number, an image. Even a tiny part of a dream may be enough to bring the message home to you. Pay special attention to what you are actually feeling when you first wake up.

Most of us need help to understand our dreams. The moment of understanding is often called the 'aha' moment – a kind of inner tingle that confirms your dream-interpretation. Share your dreams only with people who care about you. Dreams are precious because they help us identify what we really desire. They are sacred because they can draw us into closer intimacy with God. They deserve deep respect, our own dreams and the dreams of others. 'Tread softly because you tread on my dreams' (Yeats).

Your inner wounded child
There is no one to blame

You may have heard me use the phrase 'Your Inner Child' and wondered what it means. It is a way of referring to a voice within us that goes back a long way. It has to do with the little boy or girl we once were and, maybe, grew out of too quickly. When we are small, I believe, we often suppress our real feelings of anger or jealousy either because if don't we will be punished, or because we so desperately want to please our parents by trying to be perfect.

There is no end to the ways we pretended and adjusted, in childhood, to keep on the right side of our parents. At great personal, emotional cost, we pandered to their dreams for us. We would twist ourselves out of shape to fit their often-selfish expectations. And it wasn't just your parents or mine. No matter what you may think, it is true of all parents. There are no perfect ones. Parents often live out their own unfinished business through their children.

That is why we speak of our 'wounded child within'. It is often only in mid-life or later that the damage done in the early years is partially revealed. We wonder why life has gone dead for us, why we enter a period of despondency or meaninglessness. The well-documented 'mid-life crisis' is usually shaped by the kind of scars we carry from childhood. The price to be paid for the survival strategies we adopted in those early years is now revealed. It is revealed, many decades later, in the form of our addictions, our compulsions and our negative patterns. The inner child carries much power.

All of this is nothing to be alarmed about. If anything, we should be relieved to become aware of the past sources of our distress. Nobody is free from all these symptoms. We are all in the same boat. But once we can name those powerful realities of our childhood, we can then dis-empower them. It is only when we explore those early causes for much of our present dis-ease, that the healing begins. There is no need to be resistant to such suggestions, or to go into vehement denial. That way on, there is no redemption.

Whether people are healthy and wholesome does not depend on whether their childhood was happy or unhappy. Because nobody's childhood was always completely happy. No, the difference depends on whether people are prepared to examine, name and come to terms with the negative experiences of the past. And nobody escapes. But we do have the choice about what to do about it. To name it is to tame it.

The damage done by the imperfection of that first decade of our lives does not necessarily fall along a scale measured from serious abuse to minor faults. A child does not logically assess the degrees of neglect or rejection meted out to her, and react accordingly. Depending on many factors, a robust child can overcome some shocking childhood conditions, while a more fragile child can be emotionally damaged by a relatively minor moment of a parent's forgetfulness.

All of this is not to make anyone anxious or guilty but to address a desperately common reality. Many of our local therapists, counsellors and spiritual guides will attest to the reality of this condition among us. All of us are affected by our inner wounded child. The good news is that this same child, once we hear her cries, will transform our lives in ways we never thought possible. She will become our saviour. All we have to do is to listen to her, play with her and love her.

Running on empty
Do you panic when the well runs dry?

Are you somebody who works better under pressure? Do you like deadlines? Are you at your best when a result is needed immediately? Or do you prepare well in advance? Are you one of those who send out your Christmas cards in November? One of my many panic-buttons has to do with weekly deadlines and expectations around articles and talks that I have contracted to do. That presumes that I have time to sit and reflect on some of our daily experiences, and then explore some of their deeper meanings. This, of course is exactly what I try to do. It is what every priest, vicar, minister, reader, elder, speaker across our land tries to do every week.

The bother is that so often the well runs dry. There is no more time or maybe energy left. It is something like 'writers' block'. That is when I reach for my 'panic-button'. Most of you must have some idea of what this feeling is like. I'm at the end of my rope. For many of you, too, I'm very sure that the emotion of panic is never very far from your common experiences.

It may be about some big plans for the future of your family that have just been scuppered, or it may be how to juggle the ordinary, repetitious, relentless demands of each day – a child is suddenly sick, your teenager has not telephoned and it is now well after midnight, you have a meal to prepare for visiting friends but your mother is ill, your husband is late back, the car is broken down and you now have the flu.

Panic-attacks come in various shapes and sizes. They are never pleasant. People in all walks of life are prone to such experiences. Anxiety regularly weakens me when I think my wells are running dry. I have no more left in me. All my creativity is gone. I have nothing of value to say to people this weekend. There is nothing of worth that I can have ready for my next page or reflection. This distress is not a pleasant place to be.

How do people cope with those waves of panic and anxiety sweep over them? I marvel at the resilience of parents who press on relentlessly in the face of huge challenges, who look on the bright side of things when the darkness is near enough, who still get up in the morning, wake and dress the children, prepare breakfast, and drive them to the bus or to school, even though their own hearts are breaking, for one reason or another.

From where do you get your energy when you're running on empty? These days and nights, to keep sane and balanced, I survive only by handing my life over to God, or to the Mystery of Creation, to the Source of Existence. I follow Jesus in surrendering all that I am into the safe hands of Providence. Otherwise I could not face the days and nights of my life.

My mother used to say to me when I was a small boy, 'When you have done your very best, God looks after all the rest.' In other words, give life your best shot, and never be anxious, fearful or depressed. The Good Book reminds us that 'I can do all things in him who makes me strong.' This belief never fails to fill me with energy, life and light.

When panic strikes me now, I pause for a few deep breaths, I relax my shoulders, and I call in the angels of my life. I do believe that I am deeply loved by a Tremendous Lover, who guards and protects me as the most loving of mothers do. To know that you are extravagantly loved by the most powerful and beautiful of all the gods and godesses – the God of Love itself – cannot fail to fill you with a new smile, a new heart, and a new spirit of energy.

Forever young
Memories that bless and burn

In Summertime we dream. The warm winds comfort our hearts. Long evenings are for memories that bless and burn. There is often an ache within us when we look back on our lives. It happens a lot to me in mid-Summer.

During these weeks of July I carry a kind of nostalgia; I remember, with strange and elusive emotions, the playful days of childhood. 'Where,' I now wonder to myself, 'have they all gone?' What has happened to that part of me that loved to laugh and play all day long? That part of me that could not wait to go barefoot on the first warm day in May, and stay that way all through the hot Summer? That part of me that could not wait for the dawn to come because there were so many games to play, so many things to do, so many mysteries to discover? Even as I write this, I can still feel in my body that aching call to explore the darkness of the small woods around our village.

I loved being young and new. I loved being beautiful and perfect. I was excited about something every day. I was always happy then. The whole world was my playground. 'Any reason was a good enough reason for you to celebrate,' my Mom once told me when I asked her about what I was like when I was small. My heart still melts when I read Dylan Thomas' *Fern Hill*:

All the sun long it was running, it was lovely.
The hay-fields high as the house,
the tunes from the chimneys;
it was air and playing,
lovely and watery,
and fire green as grass.
And the Sabbath rang slowly
In the pebbles of the holy streams ...'

When I was about seven I won famous victories with my two loyal companions and my lightening-fast pistol-draw. Time and time again we defended our village, shooting the bandits and slaying the evil dragons relentlessly until my mother called us home across the fields before the dark. We named ourselves 'The Tough Trio' and we had our own secret code-sign: with thumb and forefinger of the right hand we flashed a silent 'C' to each other, from hidden places, to signal the beginning of yet another rescue-mission. We were heroes then. Long before Superman and Spiderman were born (were they born?) we had saved the world many times.

    Now I was young and easy under the apple boughs
    about the lilting house and happy
    as the grass was green.
    The night above the dingle starry.
    Time let me hail and climb
    Golden in the heydays of his eyes.
    And honoured among wagons, I was
    prince of the apple towns …

I think we shine like God when we're small. We carry God's delight into all our adventures. But something happens when we grow up. The light in us dims. The dream dies. Everything becomes ordinary. The magic fades.

And yet, our inner child remembers. Unbelievably, there is a magic to be worked at any decade of our lives. I have no doubt now that the excitement and the encounters with light and darkness of our childhood years can be recovered, re-lived and re-joiced in. There is an eternally young child in all of us, who still jumps out of bed, impatient for the day to begin; who still wants to be a hero and win the world from evil; who still believes that a fairy-prince will kiss her into her true beauty; who still believes that there's more to life than the cultural and religious boxes in which we live.

Last Saturday at our School/Parish Family Day with its happy crowds of face-painted children, I appeared on the rooftop as Spiderman. As I climbed into the red and black cobwebby suit I wondered about my sanity! And then I remembered the words of Jesus about becoming childlike again. And I heard my inner voice calling me to stop being so damn serious and to come out to play.

I have read that if we all spontaneously did what was most urgent in our hearts, we would go barefoot, play and act the clown. Maybe its time we did.

To care for the earth
Is our sudden compassion too little and too late?

In the past, especially in certain Roman Catholic priorities, there was often a heavy emphasis on individual salvation, on 'saving my own soul', while a more universal concern was often lacking. In this third millennium of instant communication in what has been called our 'global village', the Christian churches, together with the rest of the world, seem now more sensitive to a whole range of wider issues. But is it too late?

There is a welcome breakthrough into a more truly Christian and civilised way of living our lives. We are often too narrow and too confined to our own immediate interests – our own health, our own immediate family, our own individual rights and well-being. There is nothing wrong with such pursuits. What needs to be developed is a stronger sense of how dependent we all are on each other, how interconnected and interrelated, how much we need to look beyond the horizons of our immediate environment.

It is said that when people first saw the astronauts' famous photo of that fragile and beautiful 'small blue ball' of our earth, gently turning in space, that a new sense of protectiveness and responsibility filled our hearts. We want, instinctively, to keep that planet that is our home safe and beautiful for our children.

This desire and awareness comes from a growing compassion. Compassion is a lovely word and a most powerful force. It can be described as 'accurate and effective loving'. Compassion is an almost forgotten virtue that needs to be brought back into the currency of our preaching, teaching, civic budgeting, public administration and international planning these years.

It is compassion that nourishes within us the spreading consciousness of the serious challenges to our wider environment. It is compassion that makes us outraged in the face of the destruction of the human family and of our mother earth. The passion for justice flows from compassion. It stems from a vision of peace, equality and freedom.

We can set about this transforming work in two ways. One is the personal approach – when we purify our lifestyle in humanitarian and ecological ways. The other is the way we vote, where we do our shopping, and the petitions we sign on behalf of voiceless people and of the daily diminishing but irreplaceable species of flora, fauna and fishes.

To be a responsible citizen of the world today we need to ask ourselves about how passionate is our concern for what lies outside our immediate corner of the world. Where, for instance, do we stand on local, national and international issues to do with racism, sexism and the plight of third world countries? And how much of our time do we devote to fighting against the manipulation and exploitation of poor people and of rich forests and soil?

Today's headlines focus on the wholesale collapse of our world economy and of our few personal savings with it. In our preoccupation with personal sins we have been blind to the greedy, stealthy monster of the far more corrosive institutional sin. This sin, as we know to our sorrow, is alive and well, and lives and lurks in the heart of many of our huge international companies, our huge military and monetary systems, and even in the churches themselves. This subtle, corporate, insidious darkness is far more difficult to pin down and dismantle than the personal sins we commit seven times a day. It is only our compassion that will find the light in those shadows.

The leper in the heart
Befriending and holding the Untouchable

As I write this I'm living in Ripon, North Yorkshire. There is an old Leper Chapel in our parish. As Dean John of our cathedral recalled the history of that amazing place, I could almost visualise the congregation of untouchables that crowded into their small haven, nearly one thousand years ago.

Braving the dangers of forests, weather and bandits, assorted groups of travellers, lepers and pilgrims to St Wilfrid's shrine would have crossed the river Ure near the present North Bridge. Then, desolate and desperate, so many of them would have crowded into the hospital of St Mary Magdalene just outside the north gate of the city.

The chapel and the hospital worked together. Priests, sisters and brothers were fearless in the face of the dreaded disease. Our city should be so proud of them. There is a Leper Window in the Oak Rood Screen that divided the sanctuary from the rest of the chapel. Through this window the segregated lepers could watch what was happening on the other side, and reach through, with their disfigured hands, to receive the balm of Holy Communion. What a heart-rending scene that must have been!

I do not know why this kind of memory affects me so much. It has to do with 'the tears of things'. Maybe there are lepers in every society. Maybe there is a leper in each one of us. Anyway, only the Leper Chapel remains today. It is on the fringe of Ripon. Such places are always on the fringe of things, on the edge of our city-centres.

Maybe this is the way it has to be. But maybe not. We tend to push what is unpalatable and different to the periphery of our public places. It is easier to handle what is threatening and disturbing when it is pushed to the boundaries of our lives. We do the same thing with those parts of ourselves that have a hint of difference and darkness. We prefer not to have to look too closely at those dark things that flit across the fields of our minds each day.

There are many kinds of leprosy. And they are all around us.

They are within us, too. The leprosy we carry deep in our own psyches is probably the most subtle and powerful of all. What are the names of these subtle shadows that we banish to the leper chapels on the fringes of the city of our souls?

What about the resentment towards someone that has lodged in our hearts for a very long time? Or the things we did in the past that we prefer not to face anymore? Or the smouldering anger, the persistent envy or jealousy, the guilt or shame that we are afraid to deal with? Or the abused child within who wants to be called by name? Can *you* name your own particular lepers?

This naming of our shadows is a notoriously difficult thing to do. But there is a real danger in not naming them. If we don't name them, they come to life in someone else! Hermann Hesse wrote, 'If you hate a person, you hate something about him or her that is part of yourself. What is not part of ourselves does not disturb us.'

When we resist naming the distorted parts of ourselves, we name and blame them in others. What we refuse to recognise deep within, we project out to those around us. We scapegoat them. And we hate them. We do not want to meet them. That is why we banish them to the fringe of our lives, to the Leper Chapels of our city. What pleading hands are reaching out to you, from within, through the Rood Screen of your forgotten childhood, to receive the Holy Communion of your recognition, acceptance and healing?

In praise of leisure
What am I doing with my one wild and precious life?

School's out. The pupils are children again. The city resonates with their presence. Since this is the month for asking silly questions, I have a few. Do we need to keep these young ones cooped up all day, every day, following a curriculum devised by intense adults? A close friend of mine home-schools her three children, 13, 10 and 5. I met up with them all recently. They are delightful kids, friendly and intelligent. They have a wonderful time with their parents. They learn what they need to know, for a full and rich life.

As one who started going to school at a ridiculously early age, and stayed there for two decades, I have often wondered why we submit the vast majority of our children to the relentless, daily regime of an exam-filled life from four years of age to eighteen? There must be another way to learn, a way that is less threatening and less demanding. Before you begin to argue, I just ask you to reflect a little on the question I ask. (Harassed parents need to learn that play, far from being a waste of energy, is where the greater part of a child's mental and emotional development takes place.)

And there's more! I have the same kind of difficulty with our lives as adults. Was life really meant to be packed with work from morning till night, sometimes for seven days a week? We long for our summer holidays, for a Sunday afternoon stroll in our lovely Market Space, for retirement – so why do we not insist on a national system that provides more free time, more Bank Holidays, more space just to be? I have heard many elderly or dying people wishing they had spent more time playing with their children or grandchildren or just simply *being* rather than *doing*: but I have never heard anyone regretting not having spent more time cleaning, washing the dishes, or working in the office or factory! When the French awarded themselves a 35-hour week a few years back, communal enthusiasm and productivity rose rather than fell. Maybe you love working. If that is so then you must think that what I'm saying is simply naff, and really, for the birds.

Talking of birds, did Jesus not remind us about the way they live their lives – free from anxiety and full of trust? Likewise with the lilies of the field, who neither toil nor spin. Above all Jesus adored children, and held them up as role-models for adults in their carefree play and their non-addiction to work. And have you ever noticed the way a sheep or a cow looks meaningfully at nothing in particular – in a superior and contemplative kind of way? 'What is this life if, full of care, we have no time to stand and stare. No time to stand beneath the boughs, and stare as long as sheep or cows?'

More and more people are doing this. They are deciding to slow down. They are beginning to ask themselves the question, 'What am I doing with my one wild and precious life?' They are reducing their work hours, taking less pay, retiring earlier. Their health is improving, their marriages are stronger, their links with their families more life-giving. Less worried about life after death, they are reaching for the abundant life before death.

'One day people will touch and talk easily. And loving will be natural as breathing, and warm as sunlight. And people will untie themselves, as string is unknotted; they will unfold and yawn and stretch, and spread their fingers; they will unfurl, uncurl like seaweed returned to the sea; and work will be simple and swift as a seagull flying, and play be as casual and quiet as a seagull settling; and the clocks will stop, and no one will wonder, or care or notice; and people will smile without reason even in winter and in the rain.'

Miracle on the motorway
Doing what you love or loving what you do?

Some of us hate our work. Some of us love it. Perhaps, for most people, it is a love-hate transaction that sometimes gives us job satisfaction and other times we just want to stay in bed. Much depends on our general approach to life and to God. The lucky ones, I feel, are those who believe that everything they do has a wider repercussion; that no action stands on its own, but is connected with everything else.

Here's an example I often use when talking about their work to teachers, parents or other professionals. It is called 'the infinite horizon' approach. Two men were building a wall. When the first was asked what he was doing he said he was fed up with placing bricks in a row on a boring old wall and could not wait for 5.30pm on Friday to knock off and sink a few pints. The other brickie said he was building the north wall of a cathedral. He said it with the passion and pride of an artist, and already, in his heart, he could see the magnificent edifice, an elegant and beautiful sacrament of God's presence amongst us.

The prophet wrote that 'work is love made visible'. Whether washing the dishes, driving a taxi, delivering the post, sitting at a check-out, ferrying the children all over the place, looking after an ill member of the family – everything can be seen as having a richer meaning in terms of the common good, of building community, of contributing to a happier neighbourhood. Even the trivial things we have to repeatedly get done are all an essential part of the bigger picture. Nothing is wasted and everything is harvested when we see what we do against an infinite horizon.

This vision of the interconnectedness of everything also means that we develop a happier attitude to our daily work. A kind of sacred dimension can enter in to what we once regarded as a boring old job. We can lessen the deadly effect of routine on our souls, and find a freshness in what had become stale and jaded. 'In the middle of my Winter I found an invincible Summer.'

You may think that this kind of attitude is fanciful, unreal or plain stupid. But think again. There are millions of workers, many of whom subscribe to no religion, who pause for a few minutes each morning to reflect on the wholeness and holiness of what they are about to embark on that day. They fill themselves with a sense of respect for those they will encounter, and a sense of the dignity of the day's work they are about to begin.

Such people, whether they work in offices, in fields or at home, see themselves as different kinds of artisans and artists, creating something beautiful for the world and for God. As with Mother Teresa of Calcutta, this approach is meant to be at the heart of every Christian's life. It is not an easy skill to master. We need help to understand the depth of our various vocations and to read our lives in this loving way. To achieve such a deep presence to the world around us is why God, in the first place, wished to be fleshed, why Jesus loved to hang out with us, why we pray, and why we celebrate the eucharist.

When we begin to believe this transforming vision of work and try to put it into practice, one of the first things that happens is, we start paying more attention to what we are doing. We attend more carefully to the details of our daily labour. No matter how ordinary the job, we see what we are doing in a wider, deeper context.

In this regard, I have been deeply influenced by a man I never met. Morning after morning, through the seasons of our unpredictable weather, I have watched him gather up the crashy remnants of other people's carelessness. I have watched him restoring dignity and destiny to the most menial type of labour. In this small poem I have tried to capture his silent witness.

Empty Monday faces behind wet windscreens,
inching their grim way along the A64 into Leeds.
The work that awaited, was already destroying them.

And then I saw him, as I see him almost every day. On the verge
of the soulless carriageway, his face is beautiful with attention.
He is holding the details of his day against an infinite horizon.

Like a mother to her baby or a cellist to her instrument,
like a painter to his canvas or a priest to his altar,
the litter-picker, with meticulous dedication, stoops carefully
to renew the face of the earth.

About men (and women)
Spare a thought for us males!

A recent and significant piece of research by the Mori Institute found that most men between 35 and 55 were 'cynical, jaded, suspicious of authority and fed up with the rat-race'. They said that they were disappointed, miserable, disillusioned and felt negative about almost everything. This surprised me but maybe it is unfortunately true. Men, it seems, do not, after all, have everything their own way. There is another side to the story.

I was down near Glastonbury last week giving a men's retreat. Did you know there were such things? It was for men only. It quickly emerged that men, as well as women, are abused and victimised in our current structures and cultural values. Men, as well as women, need liberating from the tyranny of expectation to succeed at work, to prove their manly worth at many levels, to compete and win in every rat-race in town.

A big part of the current malaise among men has to do with relationships. When it comes to communicating and relating, men, as John Gray insisted in his famous research, are from Mars; women from Venus. Many pressing questions were asked by those who attended the reflection day. With such a challenging theory is there any chance of true and lasting harmony? To what school do we go for lessons in mutual understanding and communication? Given the gender differences in our human make-up, is it not extraordinary that so many couples manage to keep loving each other for so long?

After a bad day, for instance, when spouses or partners meet, there is, apparently, a marked difference in their expectations. The man, for instance, wants to be left alone and may leave the kitchen for the isolated tool-shed to work the thing out, somewhere or other, on his own. There is a solution to be discovered, a plan of action to be decided upon. That alone is important – how to solve the problem immediately, to find the answer. Women, on the other hand, desire to be listened to as they share their emotions. They do not, apparently, want quick-fix solutions – they want their story to be heard, their emotions around the day's experiences to be understood. The action can wait for another day.

Men, it became increasingly obvious, are from Mars when it comes to this 'Venus world' of women. At the retreat we discussed a fairly recent survey of divorced and distressed women, about the cause of their trouble with their partners. The central issue concerned the fact that the men in their lives were either unable or unwilling to explore and express their own personal emotions. In short, they were either unable to experience their deep-seated feelings or, once aware of them, to share them with their chosen partner. This was something that women found to be deeply divisive and divorcing.

In the course of our conversations, some other pressing realities came to light. There is a simmering anger in many men. It is generally accepted that this emotion is predominant today in the male psyche. When explored and expressed, what then emerges is a deep-seated grief beneath the anger. It is the need to mourn, at a raw kind of level, that we males need to take on board. Another potentially disruptive theme about the planetary differences between women and men concerned the issue of talking and listening. Some research or other reveals that women use five times more words than men. For many men, apparently, this constituted a serious a threat to their relationships and marriages.

Yet another debilitating difficulty arose to challenge the male ego and his self-esteem. Traditionally regarded as the 'breadwinner', men now struggle to find another self-definition, since so many are out of work. To add insult to injury, age discrimination is no longer confined to those over 50. According to recent research by Third Age Foundation, job seekers in their 40s are excluded from work because employers regard them as 'over the hill'.

We finished our retreat with more questions than answers; but to ask a good question is often more important than to find an incomplete answer. By its very definition, this retreat-experience was all very one-sided. I cannot help wondering how a group of women would address these, and similar issues.

The 'morning' person
Do you remember saying your 'Morning Offering'?

Are you a 'morning person' or an 'evening person'? We all know those who are lethal until they've had their first cup of coffee or first cigarette. We know those, too, who are empty of energy, creativity and goodwill by the time the sun sets. We are such complicated, sometimes unpredictable, human beings. Some of us are at our best in the morning; others blossom in the late evening.

The purpose of this reflection is to suggest that what we think, do and say first thing each morning will influence and colour the rest of that day. Most people who try to live their lives deeply, wisely and compassionately, find that the morning is the best time to spend those 15/20 minutes in some kind of prayer or silence. (I really think the time has come when busy men and women realise that it is little short of psychological or spiritual suicide to try to hold the burden of our humanity, without some quiet reflection-time.)

What we do in the morning affects the rest of the day. When I was a child we were taught to 'make our Morning Offering'. It was a kind of statement of intent. The whole day was promised to God. Even when we would forget to think explicitly about God, nevertheless, our dawn promise would hold true. Once we managed to get it right after we woke up, then everything would be right all day.

St Paul reminds us of the importance of filling our minds and hearts with all that is good, beautiful, loving and compassionate. Because as we begin, so shall we continue. Most of the great religions are clear about the need for a good start to the day. In his lovely book *Sabbath*, Wayne Muller quotes an old Hasidic poem:
Take special care to guard your tongue before the morning prayer.
Even greeting your fellow, we are told, can be harmful at that hour.
A person who wakes up in the morning is like a new creation.
If you begin your day with unkind words, or even trivial matters; even though you may later turn to prayer, you have not been true to your Creation.
All of your words each day are related to one another.
All of them are rooted in the first words that you speak.

Dear Reader, please do not grow tired of my insistence on the power of those few minutes you try to set aside each day, to recollect yourself, before plunging into the demanding deadlines of the day ahead. (Have you noticed how our best athletes, just before they begin their run, jump, game or test, will often pause with eyes closed to set the scene, to gather the distracted pieces of themselves into their centre, to focus their concentration and energy?)

Even when we start the day with the best of intentions, it is still so easy to become separated from our true heart. We are born for 'right living' but we are soon tempted. We genuinely want to be good, to pursue true beauty, but we are quickly distracted and seduced by false attractions. We find ourselves betraying our best nature in all kinds of ways. This happens when we lose contact with our trustworthy hearts. The recipe for our wholeness and healing is written on them. 'Where do we begin the journey of each day of our lives?' the famous mystic Eckhart was asked. He replied, 'Begin with the heart.' And when we were small, my mother was for ever reminding us: 'This above all – to thine own self be true; and it must follow, as the night follows the day, thou canst not then be false to any man.' (*Hamlet*, Act 1, Scene 3)

De senectute
Do you really believe that the best is yet to be?

Now that I'm in my sixties, I'm feeling my age. Everything reminds me that I'm on the last lap of my life. These mornings, for instance, as Winter scribbles white messages on the presbytery window panes, I feel the cold as never before. My bones creak. No longer can I leap from my bed as I once did. Yesterday I tried it, and now those worrying dizzy spells have returned. I look at my body (from a safe distance!), and wonder what has happened to it.

But it's not all bad news. As well as being depressing and threatening, growing old can be exceptionally pleasant too. From mid-life onwards, a new freedom often sets in. There is nothing more exhilarating than to wake up each morning without fear, and to go to sleep each night without an anxious ache. For much of our lives, like a shadow-monkey on our back, we worry about proving ourselves better than others, about staying ahead of the pack, about pleasing somebody or other. Now, however, there is the possibility of living 'the abundant life' with renewed energy.

In recent years I have increasingly felt the need to gather together the strands of my life, to shed the fat of it, to try to simplify and refine it. 'What is the most important thing in my life right now?' I asked myself; 'Of what really unnecessary baggage can I at last let go?' These are vital questions. While there is no guarantee that increasing age brings increasing contentment, nevertheless, undoubted graces become available as we advance in years.

As I visit the elderly in the course of my work, I cannot help but notice the depression of so many. It is quite sad to see their last decades filled with unhappy memories, unfulfilled dreams, and feelings of bitterness over the unfairness of life. What is to be avoided, in later life, is a submissive and defeatest mentality that longs for a passive end to the challenges of life, that seeks a final struggle-free emptiness.

No! The goal of getting older is to keep the fire in our bellies burning; to do more truly important work because now we can

119

choose it, because now we are free. It is to be more creative and passionate because we have less to lose. It is the time for fulfilling the hopes and dreams we always carried, but hidden under the pressures and stresses of coping with life and of providing for our families. 'What! Me retire?' exclaimed Samuel Beckett in his nineties. 'How could I retire with the fire in me now?'

'The best is yet to be.' Every decade of life, especially the later ones, brings new fields to be furrowed and ploughed, with seeds to be set and a harvest to be gathered. Around the so-called retirement decades we should have the expectation for exciting new doors to swing open, not slam shut. Previously unreachable horizons now seem attainable, after all.

In the last quarter of our lives we travel leaner, loser and lighter. We find ourselves stripped of titles and offices and importance. Feeling empty and fairly vulnerable, we have time to think about what we have become, and how really useful our lives have been. Then, one morning, in the middle of our spiritual stock-taking, we wake up to a new awareness of who we are. With astonishing clarity, we discover the few things that are really important – to be grateful for the miracle of our grandchildren, to notice the way the leaves are falling this autumn, to help somebody every day, to enter more fully into the precious mystery of our approaching death. And just in time, we may then become nothing more or less than our true, authentic selves. And that is everything; it guarantees our place in heaven.

In praise of wilderness
Beware of the tyranny of tidiness!

Outside my window there's a small jungle. Just a few trees, some bushes, a very modest hill and a few hidey-holes here and there. Parents who collect their infants and toddlers here at the church will know the place well. The children love this opportunity for adventure. In this magic place they become explorers and hunters. They celebrate mighty victories over insurmountable forces. Last week I saw Ben declared King of the Jungle, the saviour of the inhabitants and the champion of the fiercest of the animals.

Carefully manicured gardens and flower-beds don't have the same appeal for children. And, indeed, I have known adults, too, who insist on keeping spaces of wilderness close to their houses. It is a way of allowing growing-room for the wildlife in both the environment of their homes and of their souls. There is a wild man and a wild woman hidden beneath the respectability in all of us. Can you remember ever doing something so out of character that it shocked both yourself and others?

Maybe it isn't such a bad idea, after all, to allow an uncultivated wilderness to grow in our souls. We need a place to hold the chaos of our lives. This is a kind of sacred space, a space where the 'pearl of great price' often lies hidden. There is a certain splendour in such untamed places. Everything there is allowed to be different. There is no uniformity in this un-manicured place. There is no judging here, no examination, no comparisons. Everything has its own place, its own beauty. Weeds, too, can assert their dignity as wild flowers. (It has to be noted, here, that readers of a perfectionist or demanding disposition will always find it quite difficult to grant themselves permission to have such an 'imperfect' wilderness-patch in the garden of either their homes or their souls.)

This wee jungle gives a habitat for all the mysterious creatures that wander in and out of our minds and hearts at unsuspected times. There will always be an unknown dimension in our deepest being, that x-factor that will forever remain unnamed. Perhaps that is the sacred quality, often wild and wonderful,

that most resembles God. Many of you may be acquainted with
the poems of the Jesuit priest, Gerard Manley Hopkins. In
Inversnaid he longed to break free from the controlling clerical-
ism that placed borders around the landscape of his heart.

What would the world be, once bereft
Of wet and wildness? Let them be left;
O let them be left, wildness and wet;
Long live the weeds and the wilderness yet.

There is a real danger in trying to become too pure, too perfect, too neat. A place without shadows is harsh like a desert.
With no shadows there can be no colour. There are times in our
lives when we can only face the burden of our being from the
vantage-point of a dark, unpatrolled untidiness. Every now and
then we need to be able to visit a place where it is all right not to
be perfect. At the end of the day we are called to be authentic,
not perfect.

In a brief but chilling parable, Jesus tells us about the exor-
cised devil who returned to the person he had formerly possessed. He found that soul to be clean and neat, swept and tidy.
So he enlisted seven other deadly demons even more wicked
than himself to lay siege to, and then inhabit that spotlessly
manicured place. What is the moral here? 'Don't try to be too
perfect; just be your own precious, wild and authentic self.'

Everyday royalty
Remember to honour the stars of your life

Prince Charles has come and gone. Our city shone that morning of his visit. There were times, during the previous days when, in spite of a cold and wet Autumn, it felt like Spring. And there were times, too, even though we live in a city, it felt more like life in a village, a long time ago. There was an excitement in the air, as when a small community welcomes back home its favourite son or daughter. The Town Hall and adjacent shop-fronts were getting a lick of paint, the Market Square, still holding its Summer flowers, a tidying up, and the ever-busy cathedral was the venue for various rehearsals before the royal visit. It is this unsophisticated delight in its unique heritage that is at the heart of the city's attraction. There is an unconscious grace and a simple elegance about the place at times like this.

As I reflect on the careful preparations for our royal guest, I cannot help looking into my own heart and wondering about how welcoming a place that is for the special princes and princesses of my own personal life. Citizens took time off to create a worthy atmosphere for our unique friend. But do I know how to forget my own concerns, so as to have some free space in my day and in my spirit for those who, by their love, have made me who I am today? When do I pay tribute to the loyalty of those who have always believed in me?

Yesterday was a magnificent moment in the long life of our city. The Prince was made to feel special as we celebrated his presence in our midst, and thanked him for his interest, past and present, in the affairs of our community. The grace of God is in such courtesy. How often, I wonder, do we pause to gratefully celebrate those other royal stars of our lives who have never ceased to believe in us, to encourage and support us in our darkest times? These human angels have walked with us when we faltered, guided us when lost, lifted us when we fell. But we often forget to honour them, to pray for them. I adapted this poem by Tagore as a 15-minute meditation for you to do. While reading it slowly, just let the video of your life play back to you those precious hearts and faces.

Soul-friends of my life, I re-member you by heart.
It was YOU, for instance, who made me laugh one long winter,
while it was YOU, patiently, who taught me how to play again.
Some of you visited me that Winter-year when no Spring came
and helped me find my soul.

And as you crossed my threshold, each one brought a special gift:
YOU discovered my weeping, inner child, and YOU,
my lost and precious power.
YOU told me I could sing again, and YOU taught me how to dance.
Because of YOU I can trust again and because of YOU my fears
are friendly now. YOU came in the early dawn, and YOU came in the
night.
YOU brought the music into my room and YOU, the lamp.

And now, with every passing year, dear stars of my life
and soul-friends of my heart, your names are uttered
by each summer flower, each autumn leaf.
I bless you with the morning light and whisper 'thank you'
as I fall asleep

God's voice-mail

Are they tempted in heaven to go hi-tech?

Many of my friends are well aware that some days I'm quite laid back but on other days I'm snappy. One morning I'm all relaxed and outgoing; the next I'm tetchy as can be. On my tetchy days, I struggle with people who talk on and on, who drive too slowly in the middle lane, who sign their greeting-cards with an anonymous 'John' or 'Mary', who have wild tufts of hair sticking out of their nostrils, who hog the footpath when I'm in a hurry.

What makes me tetchiest of all is when, in a restaurant or pub or train, someone takes out his mobile (usually a man!) and, for whatever reason, feels he has to yell into it. Everyone stops, stares and listens. Nobody dares talk while 'The Megaphone' is tearing strips off someone back at the office, or explaining why he's going to be late home. Does he realise that none of us is interested in the details of his personal life? Does he know that he is the focus of angry vibs; that if looks could kill he'd be dead meat? Yet no one dares ask him to speak in a normal way.

Then there is the recorded message on the ansafone, giving you all kinds of options, when what you urgently need is to talk to a live person. This is getting so common. What, I wonder, would happen if God decided to install one of these contraptions? Imagine praying and hearing this: 'Thank you for calling the Kingdom of Heaven. Please select one of the following options: For Requests, press 1. For Thanksgiving, press 2. For Complaints, press 3. For all other Inquiries, press 4. (Expect a long delay when you press 3.)'

Or, they might change the message: 'We are sorry; all our residential staff of angelic counsellors are busy right now. (The week before exam-results is always our busiest time.) However, we do appreciate your call, so please stay on line. The number you are calling knows you are waiting. (After all, God does know everything!) If, while you are waiting, you would like to hear King David (with harp) singing one of his psalms, or St Elvis, belting out 'Rockin' around the Christmas Tree', please press 5.'

Then again, the message might be: 'Since this is your first call for a long time – ten years in fact – we will try to put you through quickly. For St Jude (patron saint of hopeless cases), press 6. For St Anthony (patron saint of lost causes), press 7. For St Wilfrid (patron saint of desperate Yorkshire people), press 8. For St Patrick (last resort for Irish Catholics) press 9. Please remember that we have three St Anthonys here and they are all very tetchy about being mistaken for each other.'

The last time I phoned, this was the recorded message: 'To book a reservation for yourself in heaven, enter your date of birth, your weekly alcohol-unit count, times of daily exercise, minutes at prayer, your bank-balance and National Insurance no. Then press #. For answers to nagging questions about dinosaurs, God's age, where Noah's Ark is, and the winner of next year's Grand National, please wait until you arrive here. This office is closed for the weekend, due to our annual Christmas shopping spree at the 'Trade for Change' Store in Leeds. If, however, you require emergency assistance before 9.00am on Monday, try church at 10.00am on Sunday.'

Calendar of magic moments
On being aware of everyday miracles

Mothers and fathers, what has happened to you since this time last year? Did all, or any, of your wishes for last year come true? Was it, for you, a good or a disappointing year? But, above all, have you noticed how your children have grown during last year? Have you really been attentive to the wonder of how they have changed, how they have become more mature, more adult, more independent, week by week? I really hope you have. Many parents confess to being too busy with one thing or another, to honour and celebrate the most beautiful family moments of all – those golden moments when small miracles of grace are happening to their children, right under their noses. How important it is not to miss these windows of wonder.

I do not use the word 'miracle' lightly. Your children are full of God – more full of God than we are. They are deeply spiritual. They still carry their original vision of heaven. They need you to notice all that happens to them. Not just to look at them but to really *see* them. It is easy for parents to miss the unique, unrepeatable questions of their children, the little things they whisper and, above all, the things they keep to themselves. May God comfort all those Mums and Dads who realise these truths too late.

Whatever the story of last year, you are still alive and about to begin another one. There is no point in staying stuck in past misfortunes. Our hearts are always hopeful, always wanting to trust in life, in God. Imagine the many things that will happen to us and our children as we tick off the weeks and months on this new calendar of magic moments. There will be experiences of joy and sadness, of courage and fear, of light and darkness.

Today we welcome another year. (This first day can, of course, be any day in your life.) Let it be the beginning of a 'Year of Awareness of our Children' – of noticing their shy and fleeting moments of transformation, those hidden strides of soul that they will never take again, that come round once only. And you will notice tears on your children's faces – because there is no growing without pain, no loving without grieving. And just as in our own mysterious lives, the seasons of light and shade, of joy and sorrow must pass over their incredibly beautiful spirits too. May our children's angels stay very close to them this year.

There is one more amazing thing to be said about the miracle of those magic moments in the life of your children. It is this. In such disclosure moments we see, if we are attentive, the inner beauty of a child's heart; but also, by virtue of the true meaning of Christian incarnation, we glimpse something of the loveliness of God, too. When transformation is happening in your growing son or daughter, God is becoming human again in our world. Whether your child is fascinated by the stars at night (such as Pegasus, Cygnus or Sirius), or the stars by day (such as Kylie, Will or Gareth), whether she is attracted to reading, day-dreaming or playing, whether, as a future English captain, he is scoring yet again that World Cup-winning goal or working dutifully at his books or around the house, there is no more accurate way for us to understand something of the mystery of God in our midst. It was to reveal this astonishing secret that Jesus came.

That is why I speak of the miracle of those magic moments. They are much more than 'merely human' happenings. They are windows into the nature of God's own heart. 'Speak to us of God', the cherry tree was asked. And the cherry tree blossomed.

The alchemist
How to love your enemies!

The 'begrudging brigade' is alive and well. They are to be found everywhere. Whenever I try to do something good, or different, or new, there's always someone out there who either throws cold water on my efforts, ridicules the attempt or just starts picking holes in it. I love the people who move in behind me when I take little risks to open up a new horizon here and there. These are the ones with fine souls and generous hearts. They are not small, jealous or mean. They are the salt of the earth.

I am still learning how to cope with the negative onlookers who snipe from the shadows. You all know such snipers. (Jesus certainly did!) They leave you with a persistent niggle, an irritating frustration, a desire for revenge. Such negative reactions make us unsure; they take the shine off our hopes. Here are three helpful strategies I follow to restore my inner harmony.

First, I say to myself, in a very 'common sense' kind of way, 'This issue is really not that important. My energy is precious and I'm not going to waste it on this triviality. Yes, my ego is a little bruised, but I need to get the whole thing into perspective. I do not need to become a victim of this small set-back. I am bigger than all of that'

The next thing I say to myself is a little more spiritual: 'If I try to get my own back and hit out at this awkward person, then I'm only continuing the negative cycle of bad energy. I'm simply re-acting in the same destructive way, reducing myself to the same level of bitterness and deepening the darkness. My soul, created in God's image, is greater than that. With God within me, I can let go of this small hurt, like children and saints do, and turn to where the light is shining.'

The third image I draw on is more specifically Christian. Jesus was a reconciler. That means that he took into himself all the mean and wounding things, all the damaging and vindictive things, all the envious and attacking things, and turned them into love. Like a water-filter that keeps the impurities inside and lets out only the safe, pure water of life, Jesus transformed the darkness of his desire to retaliate, and then, but not without effort, from him flowed only understanding and compassion. On a good day, and empowered by the Holy Spirit, I know that I, too, can be that kind of alchemist.

What results from all of this inner awareness, this holy work, this spiritual journey, is a huge sense of freedom. It is like a Spring day in November, a bright, warm morning after a long cold, night. But, believe me, it does not happen easily. This ability to transform our restless, unredeemed instincts is a hard-won prize. A lot of dying to one's vain ego, to the need to be approved, to the imperative to success, must be done. There is no cheap grace, no discount-resurrection.

The three golden ways I mention are challenging. It is not through study, good works, relentless church-going, crusading for this or that good cause, mechanical lists of prayers, that the crippling desire for revenge and retaliation can be transformed. As all 'Twelve-Step' followers know, we need to make that inward surrender to the Power that is mightier than we are. We need to spend those daily, prayerful minutes of total trusting and letting go into the mystery of God. Then, when we are under fire, that is what gives us our sense of self-worth and inner security. And wonder of wonders, when we realise how much we have grown because of them, we may even begin to love our enemies – the begrudgers!

Memories in wood
Celebrating the traces of our family stories

'Look' she said, 'the table is full of prayers.' In the parish house my friend was examining the small markings on the wooden table around which we were having a cup of coffee. And there, imprinted through their writing-paper and embedded into the wood, were the marks of the 'bidding prayers' that children, over the years, had prepared for the eucharistic celebration. Words like 'peace', 'God', 'love', 'help' were laboriously etched out across the grain and knots on the surface. It felt safe to sit around a table full of prayers.

My friend then recalled her own family table and how she often looked at the marks and bumps caused by her now grown-up children. As babies they would have banged their spoons and hammered their plates on this kitchen table either out of frustration at a temporary lapse on the part of Mom, or out of sheer delight at the quality of the Kellog's Koko Pops at the beginning of another gift-day for exuberant living. My friend saw those original etchings and indentations as the bench-marks of youthful growing – a kind of family album, a silent reminder of the story of their family life. It felt good, she said, to sit around a table full of memories.

Everything has a history; everything carries a story. That is why everything is fascinating. One day, at his scholarship Music School in Paris, the world-renowned violinist Yehudi Menuhin noticed an Irish boy eating some homemade bread sent to him from his native village. The great man was very taken by this special moment and he talked to the boy about the bog-oak table on which his mother would have baked her love into the cake they were now sharing. It was more than just another cake. The mother's love-filled heart had kneaded the dough into the sweet bread of life.

Three years ago we were celebrating the opening of our new and beautiful Church in St Benedict's, Leeds. In the middle of the joy we paused for a thoughtful moment. To keep the community aware of its beginnings two hundred years earlier, we took a portion of the old altar from the first church in Aberford.

Frank then crafted a few hundred crosses for people to carry
home. This is what I wrote at the time. We called it *Aberford
Cross*:

They are only little crosses, finger-length
and quite ordinary.
There is a small smile on Frank's face
as very carefully, he
hands them round like bread and wine.

These wooden splinters,
– once a chunk of altar-rails hewn
from an ageless tree and now worn down
by the weight of time and prayer –
are, it seems to me,
like sacraments of centuries.

Smoothed and grained by human breasts
at the holy moment of communion,
each cross is urgent with their secrets,
with memories that bless and burn.

So many tears in a piece of wood.

The precious stone
The amazing treasures of simple emptiness

Two families; two stories. The first family telephoned from Bradford. They were making an up-market move. The all round prospects, they said, were more promising near York. It was a calculated career-shift. The new house would be bigger than they needed but, when the financial climate was at its most beneficial, they would sell again. It was more of an investment than a home. The children, too, would benefit. They would attend a better school, live in a more prestigious neighbourhood, mix with a better class of people.

The second family phoned the same day. They too were selling their house in Harrogate, and moving to Norfolk. It was less crowded there, they said, and much cheaper to live. They didn't require all that much now, they realised, with the down-sized lifestyle they wanted to follow. They had enough of the exhausting rat-race in pursuit of success. And even when their desires were fulfilled, they still they felt empty, they said, especially now with the children away at college. It was simplicity they were after now; something more inwardly satisfying.

What a contrast, I thought. Two families; two decisions motivated by quite opposite sets of values. Neither caller asked me for my advice. But I reflected afterwards on how different we all are. And, of course, I asked myself a few searching questions. To what extent am I, like the first family, motivated by profit, success, even greed? Or, like the second family, could I walk away from all that once was important to me – my achievements, my role, my self-importance, my possessions? Am I, like them, able to travel light? At this point I remembered an Indian legend:

It was dusk and the air was still, as the wandering holy man settled under a tree, near the big rock, beside the path, at the foot of the mountain. There he would spend the night, with a stone for his pillow. He had few belongings and had long ago given up the idea of becoming successful, or of making a lot of money, or even of being popular. He had whatever he needed, and he needed very little. Now he was simply trying to find himself.

His evening meditation was disturbed by the shouts of a

businessman who came running up to him in a bit of a state. 'I had a dream last night,' he blurted out, 'telling me to come to this tree, near the big rock, beside the path, at the foot of the mountain. Here a wandering holy man would give a priceless stone that I've been looking for all my life. I can't believe that I have found you.' The holy man rummaged in his bag and said: 'Perhaps this jewel which I found today is the stone from your dream. It is very beautiful. Please take it.'

The businessman's mouth dropped open in amazement and his eyes grew large with delight. As he carried the huge diamond to his home he was bursting with pride and satisfaction. He would never see a poor day again. But the feeling did not last long and by the end of the evening he was deeply troubled. He tossed and turned all night trying to plan what he would do with his incredible richness, with all the possessions that would soon be his. How changed for ever his life would be!

But even more, something else was bothering him profoundly – he could not get his meeting with the holy man out of his mind. There was something about it that disturbed him to the core. Before dawn broke, he got up and went back to the tree, near the big rock, beside the path, at the foot of the mountain. The holy man was already up and was saying his morning prayers. The businessman laid the shining diamond before him and said, 'I have a more important favour to ask you now. Please, can I have the most important gift of all – give me the secret that made you give this precious stone away.'

The wonder of yearning
What can we ever do with our restless hearts?

My mother used to tell a story about me as a child. When asked, one Advent day, what I wanted for Christmas I replied, 'Everything, everything.' This, of course, could be the result of plain greed. I prefer, however, to see it in terms of our capacity for achieving the impossible dream, of the huge possibilities we carry in our hearts.

Robert Browning wrote 'Ah! but a man's reach must exceed his grasp, or what's heaven for?' We are full of a yearning for what is beyond us. There is a deep desire to be more than we are, to experience life and love more fully, even to be like God. We want to shine like the stars, to fly like the birds, to love like the greatest lovers. There is a lust for 'life to the full' in most of our bloodstreams.

This powerful push is in everything. All life is fired by longing. I have read that if you put a two-inch band of solid steel around a young water-melon it will, as it grows, slowly burst that steel. The same implacable pressure is found in all of nature. Everything is incessantly driven to grow, to expand, by uniting with others, to spread outside itself. That, in fact, is how the world survives and increases. It survives by coupling, by uniting, by following its inexorable compulsion to create and produce.

The human heart is no different. It is full of the instinct to reach out beyond itself, to bring joy and justice everywhere. There is a restlessness in all of us, a searching that is very hard to truly satisfy. This unsatisfied drive is impossible to ignore, to avoid or to deny. It is always there.

All of this has to do with God. God's seed is within us when we are born, the mystics tell us, and, as we grow, so does the seed. This growth is a deep fire, making us yearn for the heavens while still on earth. The relentless pressure of this capacity for, and identity with, the divine, is not only in the human soul; the whole earth, too, is ablaze with divine fire. The universe is all of a piece. This relentless yearning is written into the DNA of life as it is into the story of our inner spirits. It is God's incarnate, authentic signature. We now know that all longing is God's longing.

The sacred fire I write about is a burning and powerful urge, an incessant hunger and a strange restlessness. These basically holy drives can affect our lives in good or terrible ways. They can, for instance, lead us down the path of superficial, 'quick-fix' satisfactions, such as those provided by addictions, by our craving for sex and other pleasures, by our experiences of power, status and titles, by our escape into daydreams or institutional religion. Worse still, they can trap us into destructive pursuits when our desires for transcendence become brutal compulsions. The world will never forget the horrors of ethnic cleansing, the blood-lust for unnecessary wars, the forced allegiance to religious beliefs or to the crazy teachings of mad fanatics.

All longing is basically a longing for God. At its root, our yearning is for the fruits of the spirit – compassion, justice, forgiveness, peace and joy. God's heart beats in ours; it prays and yearns within us; it strives and groans, as St Paul reminds us, in all of creation. St Augustine, himself no stranger to all kinds of appetites and desires, reflected, 'You have made us for yourself, O Lord; and our hearts are restless until they rest in Thee.'

What strange feelings flood our hearts during these Advent days! We feel the mystery of God around us and within us. We sense the sleeping giant inside our souls. We look at the small crib-baby and see the fragile face of the Almighty Creator. God's huge heart beats in that tiny little frame. It beats in our hearts too. Small wonder that we are often shaken by storms of emotions almost too great to bear! We carry deep inside us, God's passion for the possible. The Longing that gave birth to the stars, the Longing that gave birth to all life, who knows what that Longing can give birth to within us?

The blessing called waiting
To have everything now, is to die

I can't stand waiting. Waiting depresses me. I don't do queues. Living in an age of instant gratification, I want it all now. But there is a hidden treasure in waiting. In fact, if you think about it, we spend much of our lives waiting for things to happen.

We wait for the morning during a long, empty night; for the Spring after a lonely Winter. We wait for our children to grow up, for our partners to change their habits. We wait for a new, loving relationship after our hearts have been broken. We wait for a husband to come home; for a sick child to come through. We wait for the results of a scan or of an exam. We wait for the grace of trusting again, after a bitter betrayal. We wait for an end to our depression. We wait for a cure for cancer. We wait for an end to our grieving; for the beginning of a new hope. We wait.

Last weekend at our Masses, tiny Kaitlin and Matilda lit our Advent candles. The flames flickered in our darkened church. We lit those candles for every faltering heart in the grip of despair. We lit them for every beaten community, unable to believe that the dawn will ever come. We lit them for our faithful mother Earth, forever fearful of another war.

Two babies; two small stars of light. We reflected that these prayerful moments of faith were more powerful beacons of peace for a waiting world than all the armies that ever marched. It is hope, not guns, that will one day save the world and heal our hearts. Powerful and unjust governments around the world have feared the evening candles burning in the windows of homes across the land. As well as being political statements of solidarity, these symbols of the exploited are saying 'We are prepared to wait. We believe that love, one day, will change everything.'

And who knows more about watching, waiting and hoping than those about to give birth to new life? What secret longings must sweep through the hearts of mothers as they await the birth of their babies! What inexpressible emotions flood their bodies and souls as they, knowingly or not, are co-creating with God a new beauty to bless and grace the precarious and often-threatening world we live in.

There are several pregnant mothers in our community just now. They are all heavily involved in waiting. I asked them what the experience was like. They tried to tell me, even though I knew what they were thinking by the way they looked at me: they knew that I would never understand! They used words like 'longing', 'sacred', 'amazing' and 'overwhelming anticipation'. They spoke about the excitement of feeling the babies kicking inside them, and a feeling of trepidation at the miracle of it all. One mother expressed relief that, unlike Mary, she would not have to ride a donkey in her condition.

They spoke of some anxiety about the impact of the new baby on their marriage, on the family and the neighbourhood. When a baby arrives into this crowded place, everyone has to move over a little. One mother described her pregnancy as a time of waiting – but different from any other kind of waiting. It is different, she said, because the gift is already there. Many think the waiting is over when the baby is born. But for the mother-to-be, the miracle has already happened.

In the Christian calendar, this current Advent season is about waiting. Before the first Christmas, there was a gathering of expectation in the world, a longing for a sign of hope. It all became focused in Mary's womb. The small baby of Bethlehem was the fruit of God's original love implanted in the first mud that became the first Adam. In a sense, it was a 15 billion years wait. But it happened. And, because God became a baby once, we now know that every time a baby is born it is a sign that God has not given up on the world, a lovely reminder that God is not finished with us yet. Every birth, after the long waiting, is another fragile but powerful candle of hope.

Peeling off the whitewash
How easily we forget that original vision

There is a story told in Holland about an old church. For many years, all those who used it, on entering, would stop and bow in the direction of a whitewashed wall. No one knew exactly why anybody did that, but everyone had been doing it for such a long time that nobody questioned the habit. It was tradition. It felt right.

One day the parish decided to renovate the church. Among other things they began to strip the paint off the old walls. While doing this they discovered traces of a painting under the whitewash on the wall towards which everyone always bowed. Very carefully, they continued peeling so as not to damage the picture underneath.

Slowly there emerged a very beautiful centuries-old painting of Christ. Nobody was old enough to have actually seen it. It had been whitewashed over for a least a few centuries. Yet everyone had been bowing to it, not knowing why, but sensing that there was some good reason for the reverence.

Gradually the story was recovered. Everyone was now interested in the whole revelation. Eventually they came to know who painted the picture, why it was painted, what it meant and why it was so special to their ancestors. They bowed, now, with a new reverence, joy and meaning.

There is a Christmas lesson for all of us in that story – a message about how we forget the reason for the fuss we make about this week's holidays and festivities. We build the crib, put up the tree, string the lights, play the old hymns, gather the families, write the cards, send the presents and maybe, even, go to church. But, like the people in Holland, most of us are not clear anymore about why we are so excited this week. According to a leading Christmas card manufacturer, only three out of their current 900 cards carry any reference, in print or symbol, to Christ. There is very little conscious faith left in our perennial celebration, just a habitual response to a tradition. We are bowing to a whitewashed wall, not knowing why.

Yet, all is not lost. Maybe it is better to come to church at

Christmas than not at all; to celebrate the season even in a purely
secular manner than not to celebrate it ever; to settle for even the
vague connection that many make between Christmas and
something really important that happened to our world 2000
years ago. Such moments are never wasted. And maybe, one
day, when the world is frightened, and desperate for salvation
and peace, someone, somewhere will remember the beautiful
painting – and begin, again, to peel off the commercial whitewash.

Here is one tiny example of how the core of Christianity was
hidden beneath one of the popular nonsense-songs of this
week's festivities. During the 16th and 17th centuries, Roman
Catholics in this country were not allowed to practice their faith
openly. So as to avoid suspicion, 'The Twelve Days of Christmas'
was written as a kind of coded list of key doctrines to keep the
children's beliefs alive, but in secret:

The partridge in the pear tree was Jesus on the cross.

The two turtle doves were the Old and New Testaments.

*The three French hens were the primary virtues of faith, hope and char-
ity.*

*The four calling birds were the Gospels of Matthew, Mark, Luke and
John.*

*The five gold rings recalled the Torah – the first five books of the
Hebrew Scriptures.*

The six geese a-laying stood for the six days of creation.

*The seven swans a-swimming represented the seven gifts of the Holy
Spirit.*

*The eight maids a-milking refer to the eight blessings listed in the
Beatitudes.*

The nine ladies dancing were the nine fruits of the Pentecost Spirit.

The ten lords a-leaping were the Ten Commandments.

The eleven pipers piping stood for the eleven faithful apostles.

*The twelve drummers drumming summed up the basic beliefs of the
Apostles Creed.*

The power of a baby
True love can only be vulnerable

A young father once said to me, 'When my baby was born, I lost my stammer.' So many family conflicts are healed, so much brokenness mended, when a baby is born. I have seen cold atmospheres melt in minutes when a baby is brought into a room. I have seen hard features grow gentle, and break into a smile, when a small baby kicks its feet and claps its hands in the purest of new joy. Such is the power of a baby.

There is the fear-filled power of a dictator and the love-filled power of a baby. For thousands of years before the first Christmas, it was the crushing control of an avenging monarch that the righteous people expected as the new Messiah. Imagine the amazement of the universe when the long-awaited Almighty God of Creation turned up as a delighted baby, sucking his toes and his mother's breast. Here was the Cosmic King of All Time and of All Space as a tiny tot in diapers, surrounded by donkey-pee and cattle-dung. After 2000 years, I'm quite convinced, we have not yet recovered from the shock.

Perennially we miss the raw meaning of Christmas. We get caught up in the pretty trappings of cribs, cards and carols, missing the radical nature of the revelation – the revelation that God's essence is perfectly expressed in the features and form of a very vulnerable baby. Superficial, sentimental or sugary expressions of the coming feast serve only to miss entirely the radical extravagance of a God, whose unconditional and obsessive love for us will stop at nothing, however dangerous, dirty or demeaning the circumstances. In our annual representations of the Bethlehem cave, it is worse than foolish to clean up the mess, polish up the manger, remove the nappy and the potty, throw in a few halos and have flying angels all over the place. As we know from Matthew and Luke, it was not like that at all.

When God became human, there was no pretending; it was not always a pretty sight; it was, in fact, the real thing – life without frills. It was also an amazing risk on God's part, something that could have gone dreadfully wrong. In a sense it did go wrong – horribly wrong. The baby who came into the world in a mess went out of it, as an adult, in a bigger mess. The infancy narratives – our Advent readings – written long after his death and resurrection, recapitulate and anticipate the mysterious moments of his amazing life. The Christmas account is a kind of resume or script of his destiny, of what was written in his stars. All those death-filled and life-filled moments add up to a nativity story of incredible love. And the small sacrament of this wonder is an infant in a manger. Such is the power of a baby.

When loving couples have a baby, they become as vulnerable and precarious as the baby of their love. The beauty they have created shatters their former security. Their lives as irrevocably transformed. But that is what love is like. It surrenders. It has no more masks, no more expectations, no more certainties. The Bethlehem baby's defenceless presence, his shocking and precarious weakness, his over-turning of all our ideas about the nature of God, stun us into silence. It is in this sacred silence, during the next few precious days, that the hard thoughts within us will melt, that the unforgiving walls of judgement and blame will crumble, that the shadows of our pride will be transformed by the light of an infant's smile. Such is the power of a baby.

Our bodies remember
The physical nature of our salvation

This particular reflection could be written after the vibrant experience of any joyful Sunday morning Mass. In fact, I'm writing it on Easter Monday. I'm still tingling from the Vigil ceremonies, the Mass of Resurrection and the joy-filled, loving hearts that gathered to celebrate. But how long will the feeling last? How do I continue to be nourished by the extravagant graces that were showered upon us during those three amazing days of mystery? It does not follow that we are in any way transformed simply by being present at the ceremonies of Holy Week or by singing the Alleluias on Easter Sunday morning. We can remain totally unchanged even after a lifetime of going to Mass, of listening to readings or of preaching sermons.

We don't have to remember everything. It would be a mistake to try. In fact it might be an idea to forget much of what went on in our churches this Easter. Then to wait, in careful silence, for the surfacing into our awareness, of the special grace or insight we most need. When we trust in the intense activity of the Holy Spirit within us, we know that nothing of our experiences will go to waste and that our hearts will remember whatever needs to be remembered at this particular time of our lives.

Our bodies play such a huge part in all of this remembering. Our bodies remember everything – they carry the voiceless, hidden traces of all that has ever happened to us. That is why they were assaulted with the splendid sounds, smells and sights of the Vigil – so that they would remember that extravagant moment. We are called to our senses again, by the church, on these post-Easter Sundays when the strong physical presence of Jesus holding the bread and wine convinces the confused Emmaus-bound apostles, and the probing finger of the doubting Thomas explores the broken skin of the still-human Christ.

The bodies have it. The experiences of Easter should be written across our bodies, too, as when the first day of Spring, after a long winter illness, overwhelms us with sublime energy and joy. The impact of Easter should be like the feeling we carry when we realise we are truly in love, or when a deep relationship, temporarily lost, is vibrantly recovered. Easter, like Christmas, is very much a body-celebration. Even in heaven our glorious, human bodies, wounds and all, will, like Jesus', be honoured forever. The Paschal Mystery is not so much something to understand better with our heads, but an experience to be drawn into, in the most intimate and holistic way – mind, body, heart and soul.

It is in the eucharist that Easter is forever perfectly 're-membered'. St Augustine, at Communion time, used to say 'Receive who you are' – the Body of the Risen Christ. There is little room for ambiguity here. What we have to do now is to incarnate into our very being, in a radical kind of transformation, the saving reality of what we have symbolically celebrated, first at Easter, and then at every eucharist – that we, too, *are* the body of Christ.

The whole thrust of the church's liturgy these weeks is to achieve a major shift in the way 'we live and move and have our being'; to actually become and 'flesh-out' in our lives the pulsing grace of inner light and freedom – not just to know more about it, but to carry it, almost visibly, in our bodies. 'Where the Spirit of the Lord is,' wrote St Paul, 'there is freedom. And we, with our unveiled faces, reflecting like mirrors the brightness of the Lord, all grow brighter and brighter as we are turned into the image that we reflect.'